ORWELL'S AUSTRALIA

Dennis Glover is an honorary visiting fellow in the school of social sciences at La Trobe University and a speechwriter for Labor politicians. He has been principal speechwriter to the two previous leaders of the federal opposition, Simon Crean and Mark Latham, and has also worked as a political adviser to John Brumby and other Labor politicians. Before entering politics he was a historian, specialising in early modern European history and Australian cultural history. He lives in Melbourne.

DENNIS GLOVER

ORWELL'S AUSTRALIA

FROM COLD WAR TO CULTURE WARS

Melbourne | London | Minneapolis

Scribe Publications
18–20 Edward St, Brunswick, Victoria 3056, Australia
2 John St, Clerkenwell, London, WC1N 2ES, United Kingdom
3754 Pleasant Ave, Suite 100, Minneapolis, Minnesota 55409, USA

First published by Scribe 2003
Reprinted 2018, 2021, 2024

Typeset in 11pt / 16pt Minion by the publisher

Printed and bound in Australia by Griffin Press

Scribe Publications is committed to the sustainable use of natural resources and the use of paper products made responsibly from those resources.

Scribe acknowledges Australia's First Nations peoples as the traditional owners and custodians of this country, and we pay our respects to their elders, past and present.

978 0 908011 56 8 (paperback edition)

Catalogue records for this book are available from the National Library of Australia.

scribepublications.com.au
scribepublications.co.uk
scribepublications.com

Contents

INTRODUCTION

Why I write

George Orwell was an English socialist and patriot whose subjects were English literature, the Great Depression, fascism, Stalinism, and the cold war. Why write a book about him in Australia in this so-called post-ideological age?

One hundred years after his birth and 53 years after his death Orwell, or Eric Blair, which was his real name, is still a constant presence in our lives. His relevance is obvious. Every day a journalist, editorial writer, or correspondent to the letters pages invokes his name to expose how our politicians bend our language to convince us that two plus two equals five. Self-styled sceptics use the word 'Orwellian' to denounce what they see as the inherent tendency of all government to bureaucratic inertia and all intellectual activity to totalitarianism. Professors praise Orwell as the greatest twentieth-century essayist while they bemoan the decline of the essay form. Former leftists invoke his rejection of communism to justify breaking with old comrades, and still-leftists praise his crystal prose to admonish our politicians for their failure to find the words to inspire reform.

In this short book I want to go beyond the usual explanations of Orwell's continuing relevance, to discuss what reading him can tell us about modern Australia. To me, George Orwell's importance isn't just his insight into the political implications of the decline of the English language (which is that part of his legacy that most people know about); this decline was part of a deeper loss he felt — the disappearance, under the pressure of coming wars, of a whole way of life, and its replacement with something shallower, nastier, prefabricated, more ideological and more politically and socially divided. Orwell wasn't against progress — especially if it meant reducing poverty and increasing the sum total of human dignity — but he wanted an egalitarian future that was built on the worthwhile aspects of the past, not one that wiped the human and historical slate clean. To Orwell this meant the retention of traditions and institutions that the tidy-minded ideologists of his day told him had no future — trial by jury, freedom of speech, habeas corpus, Shakespeare, Swift and Dickens, and even the British monarchy — in short, all those elements that constituted the 'native English genius' for liberty and creativity.

In the same way that George Orwell believed England had a great future as long as it didn't forget its past, I believe that Australia has a great future, but only if we remember what it is that has made us great. Conservatives would have us believe that what made us great was rugged individualism, British institutions, and a willingness to charge machine-gun posts with nothing more than an unloaded rifle and a bayonet. These things are part of the Australian character, but only part. Ask anyone overseas what makes him or her want to migrate here and they will tell you: our sunny skies and our equally sunny inclination to equality. The true 'Australian genius' lies in the creation of a social democracy without ideology — it's the genius that gave us the eight-hour day, mass home ownership, non-denominational public education, nation-building investment, a welfare state, free public health care, and affordable higher education for everyone with talent.

Today, however, these institutions and rights are being attacked by a determined and ideologically driven band of neo-conservatives, many of whom, ironically, justify their beliefs through an appeal to the democratic socialist George Orwell. Their goal is to undo many of the social-democratic reforms of the twentieth century, particularly those of the Whitlam era, weaken the institutional foundations of the reforming parties, and remould Australia's institutions and voting loyalties to help build a long-term conservative political majority. For some, this goal merely coincides with their brand of cynical and angry populism; for others, it provides a useful rationalisation for always supporting the Liberal Party; but for a more determined band, it's a blueprint for a new Australia where the ideal of 'the fair go' is redefined as 'a fair go against the claims of others' and replaced by the question, 'What's in it for me?' If these neo-conservatives have read Orwell, it is only the Orwell of *Animal Farm* and *Nineteen Eighty-Four*, not *Homage to Catalonia* or *The Road to Wigan Pier*.

Opinion pollsters will tell you that while Australia's egalitarian sentiments have been dropped down the memory hole by policy-makers and their backers in the press, those sentiments are alive in our suburbs and country towns. If there is hope, this is where it lies — not in the diluted and guilty social consciences of a few hundred economic reformers, but in the memories and living rooms of millions of ordinary Australians.

If the neo-conservatives are to be defeated and the fruits of the Australian genius saved for future generations to enjoy, the Australian centre-left must appeal to these suburbs and towns again. It's a way of life worth defending, and just the sort of society that Orwell believed should inspire real patriotism. In an era of national insecurity, the Australian centre-left must once again become the defenders of our way of life and political institutions — just as Orwell wanted the English Left to do half a century ago. This doesn't mean constructing new utopias or adopting a puritan disregard for the desires of the majority, as too many in the Australian left seem determined to do. It means practical engagement with the political process to construct a new left-wing patriotism that speaks directly to low-income and middle-income Australia, and builds popular support for a new era of reform based on the concept of 'the fair go'.

Orwell has two key messages that speak directly to contemporary Australians: that respecting the truth is essential to restoring the integrity of our democratic system; and that if we want to preserve our egalitarian way of life, the centre-left must get in touch with ordinary people again. Orwell developed the first message after his experiences in the Spanish Civil War, where he saw lies being manufactured to justify political murder. His horror about the notion that the truth could be invented for the purpose of manipulating whole populations became the theme of some of his greatest books — *Homage to*

Catalonia, *Animal Farm*, and *Nineteen Eighty-Four*. The second message also derived from Orwell's personal experience — this time his reportage of the universal destitution and oppression of the poor in England and the British Empire in the 1920s and 1930s. This is the theme of his earliest books — *Burmese Days*, *Down and Out in Paris and London*, *A Clergyman's Daughter*, and *The Road to Wigan Pier*, as well as some of his most acclaimed essays — 'A Hanging', 'Shooting an Elephant' and 'Down the Mine'.

Both of these problems — the manufacture of lies and the irrelevance of left-wing politics to ordinary people — were a by-product of the rise during Orwell's lifetime of ugly ideologies that substituted predictable sloganeering for serious individual thought, and accepted piles of human corpses as an everyday part of our political system. A similar phenomenon is at work in Australia today. We have a federal government that manufactured a crisis to retain power and made a fictional event the centre point of its re-election campaign. The government lie machine has become infinitely more subtle and sophisticated than even Orwell imagined. Corpses have become an almost unremarked feature of the struggle for national office. We have a media increasingly dominated by the pre-packaged ideologies of conservative commentators, whose nasty and joyless culture war is casting its dull grey shadow over our film, literature, and popular culture, seriously narrowing the definitions of accepted political opinion and intellectual endeavour. Far from being post-ideological, Australia has become increasingly ideological in the twenty-first century. We have a society that like the north and south of England in the 1930s is riven by geographical divides of opportunity and wealth. And we have a political left that in parts is increasingly out of touch with the mass of ordinary people and unconcerned with the practical political task of winning power and implementing reform.

In chapter one I outline the influence of George Orwell on Australian intellectual life since the Second World War. Orwell is widely regarded internationally as the most influential political writer of the twentieth century. The same is true for Australia. For half a century, Orwell has represented the ideal of the Australian public intellectual — independent, morally brave, physically courageous, and with a clear and 'democratic' prose style that can explain the most obtuse theorising of the universities to the man and woman on the street. Over that time the battle for ascendancy among key Australian opinion-formers has been heavily influenced by Orwell's ideas and behaviour. That influence survives today in a new generation of public intellectuals who are locked in a divisive 'culture war' that provides the backdrop to the political struggle to remake Australia.

In chapter two I outline the nature of the right's assault on the 'Australian genius' — who the protagonists are, their methods and the ugly, narrowing vision of Australia that they relentlessly push. Orwell's answer to the rise of this radical new agenda is the correct one: the swing to the right should not be met by an equally ideological and extreme swing to the left but, rather, by a rejection of all dehumanising ideologies and an attempt to become more human — to, as Orwell put it, get 'inside the whale'.

The final chapter argues that the non-ALP left must break out from behind the invisible barriers that separate the inner city from the suburbs to speak directly to ordinary Australians and join Labor in devising and selling a practical and realisable program of reform. Time is running out for us to retain Australia as an egalitarian country, and the non-Labor left can no longer be given the luxury of sitting back and enjoying the spectacle of Labor being mugged by a rampaging and hegemonic neo-conservatism. For too long the left has taken a holiday from real politics. Just as it did in Whitlam's day, it must try to understand the aspirations of the majority of the Australian people and meet Labor half way — at the point where a majority coalition for change can be formed and elections won.

There's only one way that this can happen. Australians of all classes and careers — but especially our politicians, journalists, academics, and public intellectuals — must put aside the nasty little ideologies and the corrupting temptations that are undermining our great way of life. They must replace it with a thorough understanding of the lives of the great majority of ordinary people. As Orwell tells us, this is primarily a moral task of questioning our own prejudices and getting to know others. Even though doing this meant experiencing poverty, war, and professional failure for much of his life, and led to him being shot, listed for execution, ostracised by his peers and dying young of tuberculosis, connecting with ordinary people was a moral task from which Orwell never shrank. If he could make the effort despite these dangers, so can we.

CHAPTER ONE

Australian intellectuals and leviathan

In 1943, an Australian soldier walked for five days through the jungle of Papua New Guinea to deliver a parcel to an observer operating deep behind enemy lines. Had he run into a Japanese patrol, his capture, torture, and death would have been almost certain. The parcel he was carrying was a book that his mate had ordered from New York and had just arrived in the army mail parade. His mate was a young Australian lieutenant named Peter Ryan, and the book was George Orwell's *Down and Out in Paris and London*.

Peter Ryan's youthful passion for Orwell continues to this day. The two men's lives were remarkably similar. Both were private-school scholarship boys from declining middle-class families whose fathers had died when they were young. (Ryan described his background to me as 'lower-lower middle class', conscious of Orwell's claim to be from the 'upper-lower middle class'.[1]) Both had served in the front line of an anti-fascist war, experienced imperialism at first hand, and had written books about it — in Orwell's case, *Burmese Days* and *Homage to Catalonia*; in Ryan's, *Fear Drive My Feet*. Ryan's memories of broken men asking at the family's door for work during the

Great Depression made him, like Orwell, a convinced socialist. And his experience of communist takeover tactics when he was secretary of the Melbourne University Labor Club during its celebrated split of the late 1940s made him a socialist of the staunchly anti-communist variety. Later he was to title his column in the Melbourne *Age* (edited by Creighton Burns, who claims to have become an Orwell enthusiast under Ryan's influence) 'As I Please', after the Orwell's renowned wartime column in Aneurin Bevan and Jennie Lee's *Tribune.*

We can taste the influence of Orwell on Ryan in his posthumous reappraisal of his old teacher Manning Clark; it was also, controversially, a recantation by Ryan who, as director of Melbourne University Press, had been Clark's long-time, successful publisher. The marks are unmistakeable: the delight in exposing the emperor's nakedness; the priority of truth over historical falsification; and a wilful contempt for pro-Soviet 'intellectuals'. (Ryan told me that his experience of the war, with its exposure of the best and worst in men, taught him to 'sniff out bullshit' and charlatans a mile off.) The result was one of the most rancorous, politically charged, and sustained intellectual debates in recent Australian history. That's what happens when the searing search for the truth takes hold. That's what happens when the essayist's model is George Orwell.

When Ryan told me the story of his brave comrade in Papua New Guinea it struck me as at odds with the dominant view of Australian intellectual life during the 1940s as thin, insular, and 'pre-Socratic'. In fact, it struck me as a good illustration of the degree to which Australia could boast, as far back as then, an intellectual culture hungry for cosmopolitan ideas.

Interest in Orwell remains widespread half a century after his death. The release late in 1998 of *The Complete Works of George Orwell* has boosted that interest and prompted Timothy Garton Ash (like Orwell, a witness to revolution), writing in the *New York Review of Books*, to describe him as '*the* most influential political writer of the twentieth century'; more universal than Camus, Arendt, and Brecht; more enduring than Solzhenitsyn; the supreme describer of the twentieth century's greatest political disaster, totalitarianism.[2] Two thousand and three is the centenary year of Orwell's birth, which provides a good vantage point from which to assess his influence on Australia, too. It is my belief that, for more than fifty years, George Orwell has been one of the most important influences on Australian intellectual life, and that this influence continues today in the work of our leading public intellectuals.

This chapter shows how, on both the left and the right, George Orwell has provided a moral and intellectual example to some of our nation's leading thinkers and journalists. The intellectual groupings that contend for our souls today and the questions they ask owe a lot to his example and his writings.

As I please

George Orwell was a source of inspiration for a number of young men of the left who attended the University of Melbourne after the Second World War. They were mainly anti-communists, and had had similar experiences fighting campus

Marxists as had Peter Ryan. Ryan, in fact, brought a number of anti-communists together within the Labor Club to provide intellectual ammunition for the fight. Called the Socialist Studies Group, they were deeply interested in all things to do with British socialism, including Orwell, whom they read in the *New Statesman* and in his books.

Ken Inglis, who was at the University of Melbourne after the war, was on the fringes of the group. His intellectual hero, too, was George Orwell. He rushed out and bought new volumes of Orwell's books as soon as they arrived, and remembered his first reading of 'Notes on Nationalism' as one of the most exciting moments of his life and 'Politics and the English Language' as one of the most important influences on his writing style and political beliefs. Although Inglis was later to become a professional historian and very much part of the academy, in his early days he doubled as a radical campaigning journalist and contrarian.

Like many others, Inglis was attracted to Orwell's campaigning journalism and his distinctive, direct form. He tells us that in Oxford he made a resolution to adopt the plain style of his admired writers at the *New Yorker* and Orwell.[3] After returning from Oxford, Inglis took up campaigning journalism, as had Orwell. He conducted a crusade to prevent the hanging for murder of the illiterate aboriginal circus-hand Rupert Max Stuart. Perhaps also influenced by Orwell, he adopted a nom de plume ('John Kemp') to investigate the Anzac tradition.[4] One of the obvious attractions of Orwell to the generation who fought or lived through the Second World War was his articulation of a left-wing patriotism that justified the fight against Hitler, particularly in essays such as 'Notes on Nationalism' and 'The Lion and the Unicorn'. It was Orwell's view that, while nationalism is aggressive and chauvinistic, patriotism can be defensive and tolerant of other cultures. Inglis later adapted Orwell's arguments to develop a defence of Australian patriotism based on what he saw as a popular acceptance of tolerance and multiculturalism.[5]

One who followed at Melbourne soon after Ryan and Inglis's generation was the later Hawke and Keating government minister, John Button. Like many of his generation, Button regarded Australia and especially its politics as philistine and provincial. Reading the *New Statesman*, R.H. Tawney, Arthur Koestler, and Aneurin Bevan (in his book *In Place of Fear*) had convinced him that the great political dramas were being played out not in Australia but elsewhere, by men of greater integrity and weight. The most notable influence, though, was Orwell:

> I became a great admirer of Orwell. I read his novels and immersed myself in his essays ... He wrote with an economy of style and fearless intent, but he was more than just a talented scribe. He was also a man of action who'd been wounded in the Spanish Civil War. In search of political heroes I found one in Orwell, though he was already dead and had lived and written 10,000 miles away.[6]

Orwell was one of the writers possessing a combination of thoughtfulness, imagination, pragmatism, and idealism that attracted Button into politics on the side of the democratic left.

Button's interest as a political figure comes mainly from his reputation for independence of mind as Minister for Industry in the Hawke government and his membership of the 'Participants' group, who took on and beat the authoritarian leftist leadership of the Victorian branch of the ALP in the 1960s, helping the rise of Gough Whitlam to the prime ministership in 1972. Here, too, we can see the influence of Orwell, as well as Koestler and Bevan. As a student observer, Button was conscious of the number of 'lackeys' in Australian politics 'willing to subordinate their private judgements to the dictates of ideologies, creeds, groups and factions.' He was attracted to Orwell by 'his detestation of political phonies' and 'admired his political passion for democracy ...' 'If liberty means anything at all,' Button quoted Orwell admiringly, 'it means the right to tell people what they do not want to hear.'[7]

This same spirit had animated the intellectual magazines of the 1960s and 1970s, *Dissent* and *Nation*, which helped create intellectual support for the agenda of Gough Whitlam. The latter, which had been modelled on the American *New Republic* and inspired by writers from the non-communist left, such as Edmund Wilson, John Maynard Keynes, Richard Crossman, and George Orwell, was created and edited by the economist and journalist T.M. Fitzgerald who had, like many others, been exposed to Orwell through *Tribune* and *Horizon* while on service in Britain during the Second World War. Fitzgerald was later to tell Ken Inglis that, when Orwell died, he felt like he had lost a second father. *Nation* under Fitzgerald had been one of the first publications to print the musings of Peter Ryan, in his anonymous role as 'Melbourne Spy', and had published Ken Inglis' investigative essays on the Stuart murder case.[8]

The Australian homage to Catalonia

These social-democratic, left-wing admirers of Orwell — who had been attracted by the moral force of books such as The Road to Wigan Pier and Down and Out in Paris and London — became influential figures in Australian intellectual life. But they were overshadowed by another group who were determinedly anti-communist and who were influenced by another Orwell — the anti-communist Orwell of Barcelona and after. These Australians were connected with the magazine Quadrant.

Peter Coleman, a graduate of the University of Melbourne during the Second World War who later moved to Sydney, was another of his generation who sought to live like Orwell. Inspired by the left-wing novelist Kylie Tennant and Orwell, Coleman tells us that he moved into a 'ten shillings per week broom cupboard' in Sydney's Old Phillip Street 'to find work in places that would provide material for the novels I was going to write. I planned to be a waiter in a ritzy restaurant, a gardener in a chic villa, an attendant in a hostel for derelicts, a labourer in a prison.'[9] After his flirtation with leftism and social-realist literary dreams, Coleman was to become a writer and journalist, but one motivated by a different side of Orwell — the Orwell of *Nineteen Eighty-Four* and *Animal Farm*, not the young left-wing Orwell of *The Road to Wigan Pier* or *Homage to Catalonia*. Coleman and those who were to later gather around *Quadrant* saw in Orwell — like André Gide, Arthur Koestler, Ignazio Silone, Raymond Aron, and Albert Camus — someone who understood totalitarianism and the Cold War and the moral failings of communism's fellow travellers:

> There was for me no turning again to the revolution that had confounded my adolescent years after the war. I had absorbed too much from George Orwell, Malcolm Muggeridge, Bertrand Russell and dozens of those who had been to Hell and back ... One or two of my circle in these earlier years may have still looked to Barcelona of 1937 (the anarchists) or to Belgrade of 1947 (the Titoists) or even to John Anderson's revolutionary stoicism or classicism. But the communists! It was unthinkable.'[10]

One of the most interesting things about the conservative followers of Orwell in Australia was their continuing commitment to social democracy — although, of course, to a form of it that was always strongly anti-communist. As we shall see, this was true of people such as Frank Knopfelmacher, Pierre Ryckmans, and Robert Manne. While Peter Coleman began his intellectual life as a social-democratic follower of Orwell, he later became and remains a quite hardline conservative. Coleman's thoughts on this topic are similar to those of the neoconservative American political theorist Norman Podhoretz, whose influential essay 'If Orwell Were Alive Today' was published by Coleman in *Quadrant* in 1983. Podhoretz's argument was that, had Orwell been still alive in 1983, when he would have been 80 years old (something that may have come about if

Orwell had not been wrongly overdosed with the anti-TB drug streptomycin), he would have been a neo-conservative, and not a socialist or even a social democrat.

Podhoretz's reasoning, subsequently shared by Coleman, was that there was a strong and consistent anti-socialist leaning in Orwell's thought. For instance, he was a relentless critic of his fellow socialists, opposed pacifism, and believed that socialist revolution *always* ends in tyranny. Most importantly, Podhoretz argued, Orwell's attacks on the left-wing intelligentsia of his day and his faith in the wisdom, instincts, and mores of "ordinary" people (two foundation beliefs of neo-conservatism) would have made his conversion to neo-conservatism inevitable.

While it was still fashionable for disgruntled left-wingers to remain socialist in the 1940s and 1950s, this became implausible later, as the capitalist system showed that it, and not socialism, had the capacity to improve the material standard of living of the working class. Most of Orwell's anti-communist socialist contemporaries were later to become neo-conservatives (including the Australians Peter Coleman, Peter Ryan, and P.P. McGuinness). In other words, like many once-radicals who had been 'mugged by reality', Orwell was on an anti-socialist trajectory from the very beginning. Like all futurist arguments, this one is unfalsifiable, and it suffers from being written at the height of the conservative economic revolutions under Margaret Thatcher and Ronald Reagan, after Keynesianism had been (at least temporarily) discredited, and before the rebirth of new Clinton and Blair revolutions invented a new generation of social-democratic thought.[11]

Other conservative followers of Orwell (who I examine in the next chapter), have since joined Coleman. One of the key arguments that motivates this new generation was made in the early 1980s by Lauchlan Chipman. He argued in *Quadrant* in 1984 that too many contemporary left-wing intellectuals are driven by an anti-elitist, anti-imperialist, and anti-sexist strain of thought that shares many of the totalitarian tendencies of 'thought control' that Orwell tirelessly criticised. Chipman blames this destructive development on the internal corruption of our universities from the 1960s onwards by peace studies, women's studies, black studies, and similar movements that have undermined the liberal intellectual tendencies that our universities hitherto nurtured.[12]

One of Coleman's closest colleagues at *Quadrant* was Frank Knopfelmacher. Our fullest source of information about this Jewish Czech émigré to Australia is a long autobiographical essay written very much in the style of Orwell's autobiographical essay 'Why I Write'.[13] Having escaped from German-occupied Czechoslovakia at the outbreak of the Second World War, Knopfelmacher made his way to Britain via a Palestinian Kibbutz and the Middle East campaign as a member of the free Czech forces who fought alongside the Allies. Along the way, he had become a Marxist and communist; but, upon reaching England, his views altered. In contrast to his treatment by aristocratic and racist officers of the Czech forces, the English treated him with respect. He was immediately attracted to the reality of civil liberty and freedom of discussion, through which he came into contact with *Tribune*, particularly the author of its weekly column 'As I Please', George Orwell. Orwell's weekly columns, Knopfelmacher writes, 'had a peculiar effect on me':

> Here was a man who understood the thinking of a soldier like me, who knew what it meant for a young intellectual to be in the army and in the war in the paradoxical way in which we were in it, and who understood our particular requirements. I also noticed he had all the things I was looking for in the Communist Party, but he did not have a number of the liabilities associated with being a communist. He was anti-fascist and totally opposed to capitalism, but at the same time he was undogmatic, reasonable, frank, and was prepared to call a spade a spade.

Within a year of coming under Orwell's influence, Knopfelmacher had begun to turn on the Communist Party. Shortly after, resting in his tent in Normandy, waiting to be sent to the front, he read *Darkness at Noon* by Arthur Koestler — a book which heavily influenced *Nineteen Eighty-Four*. 'When I finished reading it ... I found that all my beliefs were shattered. My defences were broken, and the suspicions which I had harboured for a considerable time seemed to be confirmed.' This was an experience shared a year earlier by another prominent émigré Australian intellectual and *Quadrant* contributor, Heinz Arndt.[14] From then on, Knopfelmacher was an anti-communist. He fought on through the war, increasingly outraged by the Communist Party and the left intelligentsia's 'loud mouthed war mongering'. 'Again', he writes, 'it was only Orwell who shared my sentiments.' After the war, Knopfelmacher spent two-and-a-half years in Prague. As with Orwell in Barcelona, he described this period as 'a priceless opportunity to study communist techniques and a communist takeover under what I might call laboratory conditions.' He adds: 'I would not trade this experience for anything in the world. It was my political university.'

By observing the destruction of democracy in Czechoslovakia in 1938 and again in 1948, Knopfelmacher had come to the conclusion that communism and Nazism were as evil as each other. He devoted the rest of his life to the struggle against totalitarianism. His identification with Orwell shines through in an aside in his autobiography: 'Risking boastfulness, I want to add that I regard this intuitive understanding of the totalitarian mentality as one of my intellectual assets. I think I have never been wrong on anything connected with totalitarianism.' Not surprisingly, after moving to England to live, Knopfelmacher was to purchase a copy of *Nineteen Eighty-Four* on the day the first consignment reached his then new home city of Bristol.

The emperor's new clothes

The desire to imitate Orwell — which, as we have seen, had gripped the young John Button, Ken Inglis, and Peter Coleman — had an even more fascinating manifestation in the case of the Belgian-born Australian intellectual Pierre Ryckmans. In a more-thorough way than any of the others, Ryckmans managed to follow the example of his mentor.

In the late 1960s, Ryckmans travelled to Hong Kong to study

his specialist field, Chinese art and literature, of which he is now, as a translator of *The Analects of Confucius*, a leading western expert. But finding himself through personal circumstance face to face with the reality of Chinese communism through the assassination of a friend by communist agents, Ryckmans, like Eric Arthur Blair in revolutionary Barcelona in 1937, adopted a pseudonym, 'Simon Leys', to write a classic account of the Cultural Revolution, *The Chairman's New Clothes.*

This book's title instantly alerts us to the source of the author's inspiration. In a later essay in *Quadrant*, 'George Orwell: The Horror of Politics', Ryckmans, who, like Orwell, continued to use the pseudonym after his identity had been exposed, tells that he was drawn to the Hans Christian Anderson tale *The Emperor's New Clothes* by Orwell's love of it. Orwell, Leys tells us, had even toyed with the idea of making a modern adaptation of the tale.[15] (But, one presumes, was drawn instead to the Aesopian *Animal Farm.*) Ryckmans was to eventually fulfil Orwell's intention to write a book based on *The Emperor's New Clothes* in his 1986 novel *La Mort de Napoleon*, in which the once emperor of France, having escaped from St Helena and having lost his emperor's uniform, slips into a life of normalcy in suburban Paris. (Ryckmans can't help giving us a cryptic reference to Orwell in the novel when, upon entering a hotel near the site of his old battlefield at Waterloo, Napoleon notices a vase of aspidistras — Orwell's symbol of bourgeois conformity from his 1934 and 1936 novels, *A Clergyman's Daughter* and *Keep the Aspidistras Flying.*[16])

Like the child who saw the emperor naked, Orwell,

Ryckmans claims, saw communist rule for what it was once its ideological clothes had been removed. This insight, Ryckmans believes, was a product of Orwell's lack of intellectual 'sophistication' (in the full sense of that word). Any simple child or idiot can see the obvious; its takes a sophisticated 'intellectual' to overlook it. It is in this role that Ryckmans saw himself when writing about China and the Cultural Revolution. His findings, he tells us, were commonplace to ordinary Chinese, and utterly banal. Like Orwell, he was simply a man of middling intelligence (and extreme modesty), foolish enough to write what many more sophisticated colleagues would not.[17]

In a later essay, 'Orwell: The Horror of Politics', Ryckmans rejected the attempt of the American conservative writer Norman Podhoretz (outlined above) to claim Orwell for the anti-socialist camp. Orwell, Ryckmans countered, opposed communism from the vantage point of a democratic socialist committed to a revolution that respected intellectual and political freedom. Orwell detested the Communist Party not because it was supposedly socialist, but because it had suppressed his beloved revolutionary workers and peasants in Barcelona.[18] Ryckmans detested the Chinese communists for the very same reasons.

Like Orwell's sympathies in *Homage to Catalonia*, Pierre Ryckmans' sympathies during the Cultural Revolution lay with the ordinary workers and peasants, who he believed had become pawns in a power struggle within the new communist ruling class. He saw the revolution as an act of Machiavellian treachery by the communist leadership, and as a lost chance to create a better society. Having been fashioned by their political leaders into a revolutionary movement bravely organising mass strikes and army mutinies, the workers and peasants of Mao's China were then denounced as counter-revolutionaries:

> The 'Cultural Revolution' had nothing revolutionary about it except the name, and nothing cultural about it except the initial tactical pretext. It was a power struggle waged at the top between a handful of men and behind the smokescreen of a fictitious mass movement. As things turned out, the disorder unleashed by this power struggle created a genuinely revolutionary mass current, which developed spontaneously at the grass roots in the form of army mutinies and workers' strikes on a vast scale. These had not been prescribed in the programme, and they were crushed pitilessly.[19]

Ryckmans obviously saw Maoism through the prism of Orwell's denunciation of totalitarianism. If *The Chairman's New Clothes* revealed the Cultural Revolution through the prism of Orwell's *Homage to Catalonia*, his follow up work, *Chinese Shadows*, exposed the Maoist dictatorship explicitly through the prism of *Nineteen Eighty-Four*. He writes:

> Rereading this book (*Nineteen Eighty-Four*), written before the People's Republic was founded, one is aghast at its uncanny prophetic quality. Without ever dreaming of Mao's China, Orwell succeeded in describing it *down to concrete details of daily life*, with more truth and accuracy than most researchers who come back from Peking to tell us the "real truth".[20]

Chinese Shadows details how, under Maoist totalitarianism the language was being politically bowdlerised, books censored, the past eradicated, and culture debased as a prelude to being destroyed. The Chinese Communist Party was re-writing its own history to downgrade the complexities of the revolution, write out the contribution of the masses, and boost the prestige and prescience of the communist leadership.[21] In *The Chairman's New Clothes,* Ryckmans had seen the Cultural Revolution even more insidiously as 'an immense effort to paste over, rub out or scratch away from the Chinese "page" the countless rich and living traces that the centuries had left on it so that on the "blank" page the Chairman could write his poem ...'[22] Ryckmans observed that in the Marxist China of the 1970s even ordinary pleasures, such as the enjoyment of nature, listening to banned music, or solitary pursuits were perceived as 'counter-revolutionary'.[23] Orwell, he believed, was right to argue that people should delight in the simple pleasures, such as the dinking of tea, precisely because they contained no observable 'class angle' — a point which Ryckmans was to make again in his 1996 Boyer Lectures.[24]

Like Orwell's attack on leftist intellectuals who dutifully or gullibly repeated the lies of the Soviet Communist Party (in his essay 'Looking Back on the Spanish War'), Ryckmans denounced the West's so-called China experts for failing to publish the full facts as they knew them — something Robert Manne was later also to do in his analysis of the left's failure to admit the horrors perpetrated by the Khmer Rouge in Cambodia.[25] According to Ryckmans, to understand the real

China you must get beneath the level of politics and the party to the people, which the western 'gramophones' (a favourite adjective of Orwell's) of the Chinese Communist Party never do. The following passage, which describes the ordinary Chinese peasants and working-class people Ryckmans met in his travels, shows the extent of his absorption of Orwell's critique of totalitarianism:

> In contrast to officials ... those workers appeared to me, in their simple human truth, as the rightful heirs of a civilisation that the new mandarins had not yet succeeded in entirely destroying. Their natural ease, their wisdom, their mixture of courtesy and craftiness, their richly expressive language — all this put these naive and subtle people in complete contrast with the unidimensional cardboard robots who rule them; more, they offered me the revelation (or illusion) of a Chinese humanity that had kept itself intact, as if protected by its very simplicity. Orwell had an intuition of this essential and secret hope, with people lacking intellectual formation (or deformation?) remaining its trustees amidst the universal nightmare ...

In other words, hope lay with the proles. Ryckmans saluted the 'young, revolutionary China, repeatedly suppressed yet constantly struggling ... On this "real China" we found our hopes: the future belongs to it.'[26]

While Ryckmans has entered the fray of public debate in Australia, he has done so only occasionally, indirectly and reluctantly, such as in his defence of the funding of the humanities in our universities. Ryckmans' politics has been largely international, and concerned with the defence of human values that are threatened by utilitarianism and ideology. His major foray into Australian political debate was with former prime minister Gough Whitlam and former Australian ambassador to China Stephen Fitzgerald, over policy towards China.[27] One imagines this very European intellectual, who delights in Proust, Balzac, Hugo, and the aesthetics of Chinese calligraphy, being profoundly uninterested in Australia's rough-and-tumble demotic political culture.

Ryckmans' desire to get below the surface of Chinese society to the real China demonstrates how Orwell's critique of totalitarianism ignited a passion for the search of truth for its own sake. For Orwell, totalitarianism had the potential to obliterate all that he loved about high- and low-brow English-language culture, from Joyce to the local pub. Ryckmans saw this not simply as ideologically motivated anti-communism, but rather as an argument for the defence of truth as truth and beauty as beauty. Ryckmans' deep love and understanding of Chinese culture (and, in fact, all high culture from Confucius to Proust) shows that he was no mere surface interpreter of modern politics. No ideologue, he could separate his wish to conserve the best of culture from political authoritarianism of the right as well as the left. Like many, Ryckmans got from Orwell not just a political philosophy but an aversion to the narrowing of our culture by political ideologies and interests. The same is true of Robert Manne and his contemporaries at *Quadrant*, Raimond Gaita and Martin Krygier.

Our common humanity

Robert Manne first became interested in Orwell as an undergraduate at Melbourne University, which he entered as a young democratic socialist[28]. In an autobiographical essay, modelled (again, like Frank Knopfelmacher's autobiographical essay) on Orwell's 'Why I Write', Manne tells of his conversion to anticommunism. He lists three main causes of this conversion: his personal discovery of the fate of his Jewish grandparents at the hands of the Nazis, which produced a revulsion to all forms of totalitarian regimes; the influence of two great teachers in Vincent Buckley and Frank Knopfelmacher; and two authors who 'were at this time of the greatest political significance to me — George Orwell and Hannah Arendt.' Orwell was the subject of Manne's honours thesis and his first published essay — in the *Melbourne University Magazine.*

At first, Orwell's appeal to Manne was his articulation of an argument for democratic socialism that was anti-communist and which recognised a link between Stalinism and Nazism. What also appealed about Orwell was his assault on the moral blindness, cowardice, thinly disguised snobbery, power worship, and remoteness from ordinary people of the left-wing intelligentsia of his age, an apt description of many comfortable radicals of the late 1960s. The lessons were rammed home in the writings of Arendt, Solzhenitsyn, Koestler, Evgenia Ginsburg, and Nadezhda Mandelstam.[29] But it was Orwell who stood out, described by Manne as 'one of the greatest political writers of our century', not for his literary ability or philosophical insight (for Manne, like many others, Orwell's writings lack poetic imagination and theoretical stamina), but because his writings displayed 'high-order sanity; anti-metaphysical, temperamental scepticism; an ear for cant; an understanding of power and its corruptions; a suspicion of utopianism; a feeling for the meaning of pain and deprivation; an instinctive love for established ways of life.' To Manne, a writer who associated with Stalinism or Nazism forfeited his or her moral authority as an artist, no matter what artistic or philosophical brilliance they had (echoing here Orwell's condemnation of left-wing writers and artists of the 1930s in two of his most famous essays 'Inside the Whale' and 'Benefit of Clergy').[30] This became the basis for Manne's attacks on the 'anti-anticommunists' of his own generation. In a series of essays in the 1970s and 1980s, Manne rounded on Australian fellow travellers, including Wilfred Burchett and those Australian devotees of Noam Chomsky who had justified the murderousness rule of Pol Pot because he was anti-imperialist.

Orwell's analysis also underlies *The Culture of Forgetting* — Manne's denunciation of Australian intellectuals for their awarding of the Vogel Prize and the Miles Franklin award to the pseudo-Ukrainian Australian writer Helen Darville. We can see in this work, one of the best-ever pieces of Australian extended journalism, the hallmarks of Orwell's style: his journey in search of truth; his exposure of historical fabrication; his revulsion at Darville's lack of empathy with the murdered Jews; and his denunciation of the moral shallowness of Australia's journalists and literary intelligentsia.[31]

Manne tells us that by the 1970s his early interest in the socialist elements of Orwell's work was replaced by an interest in 'the conservative undertow of his writings.'[32] Manne had become increasing alienated from the many non-communist left wingers who lacked the courage to fully denounce communism and could only enter the halfway house of anti-anticommunism. On 9 November 1989, the day the Berlin Wall was breached, Manne was appointed as editor of *Quadrant*—which, by that time, was a widely recognised organ of the political right, despite its origins among a rag bag of social-democrats, lay Catholic activists, liberals, and conservatives united by their opposition to communism.

It wasn't long, however, before Manne began to run foul of his old anti-communist colleagues at the magazine, a split that was finalised by his resignation as editor under rancorous circumstances late in 1997. Manne says that when he took over the editorship of *Quadrant* he was expected by many to turn it into 'the standard-bearer of the New Right, devoted to the politics of Margaret Thatcher and the philosophy of Adam Smith.'[33] Manne, by this stage, however, had become increasingly alienated from the harsh economic fundamentalism and social illiberalism of his *Quadrant* colleagues. Despite retaining his differences with the left-wing intelligentsia of the academy, he found himself in neither camp. Instead, Manne purposefully fashioned *Quadrant* into a journal in which intellectuals could engage in conversation free of the constraints of the orthodoxies of left or right.[34]

We can find the roots of this approach in Manne's undergraduate writings on Orwell. According to Manne, Orwell knew 'how dangerous for the intellectual was the adoption of any ideology. For at the point of adopting any received habit of thinking an intellectual ceases to be himself, that is, a man concerned with truth. Battling against his ideological self-immolation Orwell was forced ... to examine the moral bases of one's political choices.'[35] Manne's rejection of the left had been because of its moral blindness, its inability to see that, as he quoted Orwell in 1970 and again in 1994, 'there was something wrong with a regime that needs a pyramid of corpses every few years.' By the mid-1990s, however, Manne had begun to see this moral blindness on the right, too, as they also began to pile up human corpses. Marxism, which had led the left down a dead end to the irrelevance of arcane textual dispute within the academy, had been replaced as the dominant public ideology by the single-minded advocacy of the free market. 'Adherents of the doctrine of *laissez-faire*', Manne wrote in 1994, 'are almost as devoted to Adam Smith as the left once was to Karl Marx.' One orthodoxy had replaced another, with profound human consequences: 'the breakdown of community and family; the rise of savage crime; social anomie in the form of drug dependence, sexual barbarity and suicide; the emergence of the idea of the underclass and acceptance of the idea of permanent unemployment.'[36]

In a sense, with the end of the Cold War and the emergence of an uncaring orthodoxy of the right, Manne had travelled some way back to the democratic-socialist Orwell of his own youth. But not having any longer to fight against Marxism, he was able to turn from a critique of communism and totalitarianism to a critique of all dogmatic ideological thinking. His remarkable movement away from his old colleagues and beliefs showed, as it had in a number of the individuals analysed in this book, the very Orwell-like commitment to the search for the truth in the face of the constraints of our political surroundings and the temptations of self-censorship.

In 1997, Robert Manne's editorial direction of *Quadrant* had diverged too far for the magazine's right-wing board of management, leading to his resignation as editor. While there is disagreement over the precise cause of the split, Manne claims that at its heart was a dispute over the magazine's position on indigenous politics. In particular, the magazine's old supporters were annoyed by the publication of several lengthy articles by Manne and the philosophers Raimond Gaita and Martin Krygier, in which they described aspects of government policy towards Australia's indigenous peoples as 'genocide' and in which they supported calls for an apology to the 'stolen generations'.[37] Manne's, Gaita's, and Krygier's views on the indigenous question constitute some of the most penetrating moral judgements ever made on Australia and its history. The profound differences it opened up between them and their former conservative allies led to one of the most spectacular rifts in Australian intellectual life. In fact, this struggle at *Quadrant* can now be seen as one of the first shots in the ongoing culture wars that dominate debate among our public intellectuals today. While all three writers draw on a wide range of philosophical influences to reach their positions, the influence of Orwell is never far from the surface.

We can see the influence of Orwell's ideas on this debate through the importance to Gaita of the concept of 'common humanity', which is the title of his 1999 collection of essays. Gaita argues that the coercive separation of indigenous children from their parents could only be accepted by people who did not believe that the bond between indigenous parents and children could be as loving and profound as that between white families. Justice for the victims of the stolen generations, Gaita believes, requires us all to acknowledge that we all share 'a common humanity'. To make this case, Gaita invokes Orwell's essay, 'Looking back on the Spanish War' (like Ryckmans), in which he tells the story of how he could not shoot a man who was running away trying to hold up his trousers, after being surprised while on the latrine, because there was something about his absurd situation that made him seem too human to kill. For Gaita, this was a good illustration of his belief that there are times when we have to recognise our 'common humanity' with others, even our enemies and people whose culture is as profoundly dissimilar as that of the Australian aborigines.[38]

This same argument was at the heart of much of the Australian left's stand on the 'children overboard' affair and our nation's treatment of asylum-seekers. We may not know much about other cultures, but there are things we *can* be sure of — they love their children just as much as we love ours, and would never throw them into a wild sea without good reason, sew their lips together to make a political point, or ask them to fake suicidal depression to get on an episode of *Four Corners*.

Why did Manne, Krygier, and Gaita pursue the 'stolen

children' issue when they must have known that it would blow apart the community of *Quadrant*? We have already seen how deeply influenced Manne was by Orwell's reflections on the uniqueness and importance of truth. The same is true for Gaita. Gaita was drawn to Orwell's claim (again in 'Looking Back on the Spanish War') that the history of that conflict had been completely fabricated; that 'the very concept of objective truth is fading out of the world', and truth now seemed so relative that if a leader says that two and two are five, then two and two are five.[39] This, of course, lay at the heart of Orwell's later critique of totalitarianism and of the political misuse of language. But, as Gaita remarks, Orwell's revulsion over this possibility was not solely related to the possible political consequences of truth being relative but, rather, it expressed his philosophical and moral revulsion over the idea that truth could itself be endangered. Lies can destroy national integrity and 'pollute' our lives, as Primo Levi had written. Like justice, truth's goodness is *sui generis*. This leads Gaita onto a theme that we have already seen in Manne — the unique responsibility of intellectuals to pursue the truth.

Seeking the truth is the intellectual's vocation, which is best reached through the rules of conversation, free of the resort to rhetorical one-upmanship found in the conduct of political debate.[40] Herein perhaps lies the underlying principle that enabled Manne, Gaita, and Krygier to steel themselves to break free from the intellectual community of *Quadrant*. They believed that public intellectuals owe their allegiance to the truth, not to the ideological grouping to which they belong. It is not their task to defend a broad front of common interests, as their old allies at *Quadrant* clearly expected them to do. In fact, we can only truly understand Manne's editorship of and subsequent break from *Quadrant* by reference to this Orwell-like desire to conduct a genuinely collaborative search for understanding of the kind that he, Gaita, and Krygier had learnt directly from Orwell and indirectly from their teachers such as Frank Knopfelmacher.

Orwell in an age like this

As we shall see in the next chapter, Australia's major cultural divide today is between those who, like the *Quadrant* circle, see Orwell's critique of totalitarianism as a metaphor for the critique of all 'progressive' thought, and those who, like Manne and his colleagues, share Orwell's sorrow over the ugly and narrowing impact of all political ideologies. And in chapter three we will see that our biggest political divide is between those who support Orwell's belief in greater social equality and those who see attempts to achieve greater social equality as an impost on our freedoms. George Orwell's example and writings heavily influenced the intellectual conflicts that wracked Australia during the Cold War, and his influence endures to inform both sides of the culture wars that Australia is currently experiencing. I hope to be able to show that Orwell's ideas provide a potential way out of that conflict, and a means of improving our democracy and giving new life to our nation's long-held egalitarian ethos.

CHAPTER TWO

Politics and the Australian language

The force that protects our democracy isn't material. It is moral. It is the force we know as 'the truth'. Our decisions as citizens — in juries or during elections — are based on the assumption that the truth is being told or falsehoods exposed. In its name, we can take life in time of war; and, if our nation has the death penalty, in time of peace also. Undermine the truth and you can take away life, and get away with it. That the truth must be sovereign in a democracy has been understood since the time of Socrates, and was well understood by George Orwell. As we contemplate the shabby state of the truth in Australia in our age, it's worth looking at how Orwell reached his conclusions and how it helped him understand an age like his.

Orwell's belief that truth is the paramount virtue was implicit in his early works. In *Down and Out in Paris and London* and *The Road to Wigan Pier* he sought to uncover the truth about the poverty caused by the Great Depression. What he saw convinced him that, while most middle-class socialists of his day cared about the working class in theory, they didn't care in practice. But it was in Spain that the truth became Orwell's great theme. There, for the first time, he first saw the distorted truth being used to justify political murder.

In 1936, Orwell went to Spain to fight in the civil war in defence of the Spanish Republic against the fascist forces of General Franco. The story is told in what many believe is his finest book, *Homage to Catalonia*, and in one his best essays, 'Looking Back on the Spanish War'. Orwell had hoped to join one of the fashionable communist-aligned international brigades, but his application was vetoed by the secretary of the British Communist Party. Instead, he joined the little-known anarchist militia, the POUM (Unified Marxist Worker's Party). While fighting on a relatively quiet sector of the front line, Orwell was shot through the throat and evacuated to Barcelona for convalescence.

In the Catalan capital he was caught up in the attempt by the Communist Party to destroy the POUM — part of Stalin's attempt to suppress the revolution to further wider Soviet foreign-policy objectives. When the POUM was declared illegal, its members, including Orwell, were hunted down. Many were killed, and recently uncovered documents from Soviet archives provide strong evidence that, if caught, Orwell too would have been murdered as a supposed Trotskyist. Orwell was angered by the treatment of POUM members by the communists, but he was further outraged by the success of the communist propaganda against the POUM, which, absurdly, labelled them as fascist agents and downplayed their sacrifice in the civil war.

Orwell's meditations on his experiences in Spain produced some of the most original and penetrating insights into the nature of propaganda and the misuse of the English language ever written. By reading Orwell's essays from this period, one can track how his conclusions developed into the clichéd terms that are now part of everyday journalism and conversation — terms such as 'thoughtcrime', 'thought police', 'doublethink', and 'Big Brother'. Ironically, these terms have become the type of substitutes for thought that Orwell was warning us against, and have been used to argue points with which he would have disagreed. By going back to Orwell's writings on Spain, we can understand the key point he was making: democracy is undermined by outright lies on the one hand, and by cowardly and imprecise language on the other. As Orwell himself put it: 'bad political language is designed to make lies sound truthful and murder respectable and give the appearance of solidity to pure wind.'[1] As I will try to show, these lessons are of particular relevance to Australia today.

Here is Orwell on the subject of how outright lies undermine democracy:

> It will never be possible to get a completely accurate account of the Barcelona fighting, because the necessary records do not exist. Future historians will have nothing to go upon except a mass of accusations and party propaganda.
>
> ... in Spain for the first time I saw newspaper reports which did not bear any relation to the facts, not even the relationship that is implied in an ordinary lie ... I saw in fact, history being written not in terms of what happened but what might have happened according to various 'party lines'.

> This kind of thing is frightening to me, because it often gives me the feeling that the very concept of objective truth is fading out of the world.'[2]

Orwell's views on the danger to democracy posed by linguistic cowardliness and imprecision were well illustrated in his attacks on the poet W.H. Auden. Orwell, who had little time for homosexuals, was never well disposed to Auden and his circle, whom he had taunted as 'nancy boy' poets and 'fashionable pansies'.[3] But what Orwell really objected to were lines from the poem 'Spain', which Auden wrote after his return from the civil war in 1937:

> To-morrow for the young, the poets exploding like bombs,
> The walks by the lake, the weeks of perfect communion;
>   Tomorrow the bicycle races
> Through the suburbs on summer evenings. But today the struggle.
>
> To-day the deliberate increase in the chances of death,
> The conscious acceptance of guilt in the necessary murder:
>   Today the expending of powers
> On the flat ephemeral pamphlet and boring meeting.

Orwell read in these lines a justification for political killing:

> notice the phrase "necessary murder". It could only be written by a person to whom murder is at most a *word*. Personally I would

> not speak so lightly of murder. It so happens that I have seen the bodies of murdered men — I don't mean killed in battle, I mean murdered. Therefore I have some conception of what murder means — the terror, the hatred, the howling relatives, the post-mortems, the smells. To me murder is something to be avoided ...[4]

As Christopher Hitchens has recently argued, this attack on Auden was 'one of the few thuggish episodes in his prose', a product of 'his unexamined and philistine prejudice against homosexuality' and, anyway, inaccurate. Auden wasn't in fact endorsing 'necessary murder', but refusing to use a euphemism for it while, with a heavy heart, acknowledging the impossibility of pacifism in the struggle against the Nazis. (Orwell later apologised for his attacks on Auden.)[5] But Orwell's over-literal interpretation of 'Spain' aside, he still had an important point to make. He believed that too many writers and intellectuals were dangerous fools whose naivety could be used to justify war, lend cover to tyranny, and make political killing acceptable. Poets such as Auden, he believed, should get closer to their subject matter or write about something other than war and politics. Killing is in a special category. It requires powerful and extraordinary justification, and it should never be done in the name of ideology or maintaining power. A response based on an assessment that 'the ends justifies the means' is not enough.

As we have seen in the previous chapter, the passages quoted above had a big impact on Robert Manne and others; but until lately these aspects of Orwell's writings about Spain weren't of obvious relevance to people outside the worlds of publishing, journalism, and literature. Recent events, however, have made the lessons of Orwell's Spanish adventures relevant to us all. Orwell's arguments are about more than just inaccurate reporting; they are about the *planned* manipulation of the truth, the deliberate misrepresenting of the facts, the total disappearance of morality from politics — features of our own democracy that have become more common since the election of the Howard government in 1996.

Australia is currently in the middle of a vicious political culture wars in which the truth has become contested and politics more ruthless. Our political battles have become more ideological, our columnists and talkback hosts more partisan, and manipulation of the press by the government more sophisticated and successful. In fact, too often the media manipulators are kicking away at an open door — the whole notion of objectivity itself has been undermined and too few journalists do anything to call our politicians to account. It started with carefully planned assaults on the labour movement such as the M.U.A. lock out, which included disputed claims about mercenary armies of strike-breakers. It included the fight over the 'stolen generations', which saw the Howard government and its mining-industry-funded backers create the notion of 'black armband' history and introduce a radical and corrosive scepticism about the facts of the frontier massacres. And it reached its height — so far — with the political struggle that followed the arrival of the Tampa, when the truth was dumped overboard and human beings lost their lives as a result of government decisions. If Orwell was writing today he might well ask: have our elections now become so ruthless, our political commentary so debased, and objectivity so impossible that the era of the necessary political murder has returned? Do the ends now justify the means, no matter how high the toll? Let's look at one example.

Operation Relex and the necessary murder

In recent years, for the first time in our nation's history, dead bodies have become an acceptable part of Australian politics. They've been piling up since refugees became a vote-winning political issue in 2001. Many of the deaths have received widespread coverage — from the suicide of Shahraz Kayani, who set himself on fire to highlight the Immigration Minister's refusal to grant family reunion with his wife and three children, to the 353 asylum- seekers who drowned when the 'SIEV X' sank south of Java. In the second event in particular, the facts and the blame are bitterly contested. In this section I want to highlight two incidents about which the facts are not contested and moral responsibility easier to attribute. They are incidents that have received surprisingly little public attention despite being exposed on national television.

On 15 April 2002, *Four Corners* screened a program on 'Operation Relex' — the Howard government's operation to prevent asylum-seekers reaching Australian shores during the last federal election. The program made a number of allegations, some of which, like the supposed use of cattle prods against asylum-seekers, were probably wrong. But other allegations have gone unanswered. The program alleged that, during the attempted return of two clearly unseaworthy asylum-seeker boats to Indonesian territory, five people died — three drowning when their boat ('SIEV 7') ran aground 400 metres from Roti Island, and a further two when their boat ('SIEV X') — which had been ordered by the customs vessel *Arnhem Bay* to return to Indonesia — caught fire. The incidents occurred during the last fortnight of the federal election campaign, and have been covered in detail in David Marr and Marian Wilkinson's book, *Dark Victory*.[6]

Because these people died after navy and customs personnel — while under direct operational command from the Howard government — had ordered their boats back to Indonesian waters, a causal connection of the deepest moral significance obviously existed between the deaths and government decisions. Supporters of the government's actions may well argue that the Howard government did not cause the boats to come; that it did not cause them to be unseaworthy or overloaded; and that it did not cause them to be staffed by ruthless, careless, profiteering, or just plain incompetent crewmen. They may argue that the Howard government was returned not because it turned these boats back, but because it showed 'leadership'.

What the government's supporters can't deny, though, is that if the passengers on these boats had been rescued rather than turned back after being intercepted, these five people would not have died in these two episodes. Forcing these asylum-seekers to remain on their unseaworthy vessels was clearly an act of the utmost ruthlessness and inhumanity and, because it was done in the context of an election campaign, an example of brutal political calculation. Many of the sailors involved in these incidents had good reason to be uneasy about the orders they were given. What is truly surprising is how little public comment there was of the deaths. 'Government decisions contribute to the deaths of five people' should always be a big political story. Perhaps in earlier years it would have been. How public comment was dampened down in this instance was a tribute not only to a depressing lack of public interest, but sophisticated manipulation of the story by the Howard government's media machine. Orwell would have instinctively understood what was being done. Here's what I believe happened.

In the days following the *Four Corners* program, government ministers were publicly questioned about the deaths of the five people. Their spin strategy was to kill the story by refusing to give it oxygen or acknowledge the most basic facts and connections, even though they were staring us in the face — that five people had died and that these deaths had occurred while the navy and customs officials were obeying direct operational orders from their political leaders. Of course, just for insurance, the government cited the program as yet another example of ABC bias. According to the government, the story illustrated one thing and one thing only — that our navy had done a great job under trying circumstances. Any criticism of the outcome was a shameful criticism of our brave armed forces. So, while appearing to praise the navy, the government was in fact subtly shifting the blame to our sailors, and casting doubt on the patriotism of anyone who questioned why five human beings had to die to help get a government re-elected.

Here is a chronology of media events:

- When asked about the drowning allegations at a doorstop interview on 16 April 2002 — the day after the Four Corners episode — the Prime Minister repeated *seven times* his spin that our navy had done a great job under difficult circumstances. Ignoring the facts presented on the program, he stated that: 'There is no evidence that any action by the Royal Australian Navy has led to the death of any person.' Note how the carefully worded answer evades any responsibility on his part and how it fails to acknowledge any causal connection between the deaths and the actions of the navy. The statement even refuses to acknowledge that any deaths occurred at all.
- The next day — 17 April — the Prime Minister answered talkback callers on the Liam Bartlett show on Radio 6WF. One caller, referring to the alleged drownings off Roti Island, said: 'I'd remind the PM that three people ultimately died as a result of that, three refugees actually died and here we've got the commander of the ship saying it was the PM's call.' The Prime Minister replied by not replying or even acknowledging the charge: 'Well Liam I don't think that was a question. That was a political diatribe.' When pushed to respond, ever so gently, by Bartlett, the Prime Minister said in an indirect reference to the event 'I resent the attempts now being made to denigrate the behaviour of our navy

personnel. I'm thinking in particular of the *Four Corners* program.' First he dodged the question; then he shifted the responsibility to the navy (by not answering the charge that he gave the orders that led to the deaths); and then he attacked the objectivity of the ABC.

- When the Treasurer, Peter Costello, was asked at a doorstop interview on 16 April whether he was concerned about allegations that three people had died off Roti Island after their vessel had been turned back by the navy, he dodged the question and spoke in general terms only about the asylum-seeker issue.
- In a prepared media statement the day after the Four Corner's program, the Defence Minister, Senator Robert Hill, denied allegations of brutality by members of the navy and also ignored the deaths.
- And the Minister for Immigration, Philip Ruddock, who was overseas on official business at the time of the program, made no statement about it at all.[7]

The serious charge that government decisions led to the deaths of five human beings was cleverly dodged, and barely survived a single 24-hour media cycle. This is the type of organised evasiveness and linguistic imprecision that Orwell so eloquently warned us about. But these episodes demonstrate yet another of Orwell's warnings — putting lives at risk is now considered by some to be a legitimate gamble to retain political power. It is considered to be 'leadership'. Our political culture has become utterly debased and morally polluted. We are once again living in the age of 'the necessary murder'. Where will it stop?

Children overboard and down the memory hole

In the opening scene of the novel *Nineteen Eighty-Four*, the central character, Winston Smith, sits at his desk, hidden from the telescreen, and writes in his diary for the first time. He knows that what he writes will be discovered and that, according to the logic of 'thoughtcrime', writing in his diary — even contemplating doing so — was as good as committing suicide ('thoughtcrime *is* death'). What does he write? (The punctuation is Orwell's.)

> April 4th, 1984. Last night went to the flicks. All war films. One very good one of a ship full of refugees being bombed somewhere in the Mediterranean ... you saw a lifeboat full of children with a helicopter hovering over it. There was a middle-aged woman might have been a jewess sitting up in the bow with a little boy about three years old in her arms. little boy screaming with fright and hiding his head between her breasts as if he was trying to burrow right into her and the woman putting her arms around him and comforting him although she was blue with fright herself, all the time covering him up as much as possible as if she thought her arms could keep the bullets off him. then the helicopter planted a 20 kilo bomb in among them terrific flash and the boat went all to matchwood. then there was a wonderful

> shot of a child's arm going up up up right up into the air a helicopter with a camera in its nose must have followed it and there was a lot of applause from the party seats …'[8]

What could be more heart rending than the sight of a refugee mother, in an open boat, trying to protect and comfort a small child? But she's different from us — she's a Jew and represents a danger. Orwell was making the point that if you can convince people that this helpless and desperate mother and her child are a threat to your country, you can convince them that what's needed is strong, authoritarian — even totalitarian — leadership. Orwell, of course, couldn't have known that, more than fifty years later, a similar propaganda ploy would be used in an Australian election campaign. The Australian government may not have deliberately sunk ships (although it clearly did turn unseaworthy vessels back to sea, delayed rescue operations for political reasons and, according to some reports, engaged in sabotage of asylum-seeker vessels), but it certainly did misrepresent images of asylum-seekers in order to shape public opinion. As in the movie Winston Smith described, it is only possible to portray a desperate mother and child as a threat when that threat has been fabricated by a ruthless party-propaganda machine — when it's pure fiction, bearing not even the relationship to the truth that is usually implied in an ordinary lie …

We now know that at least two outrageous political lies were told to the Australian people during the 2001 federal election: that the parents of asylum-seekers had thrown their children overboard, and that senior members of the government did not know that this was untrue. It was an example of political ruthlessness and fiction worthy of the Ministry of Truth in *Nineteen Eighty-Four*. The episode had four main steps:

First, the government seized upon a politically convenient and garbled fourth-hand report that parents had thrown their children overboard. Within hours we were being told that these weren't the sorts of people we should let into Australia, which set off a xenophobic tabloid frenzy that had a massive impact on the election campaign. At the root of the problem was the government's belief that there was no imperative for them to determine the truth of such claims before they were repeated to the public as fact. The mere fact that the report existed *as a report* was always going to give the government the crumb of credibility it thought was enough to get away with the claim. The government could always simply blame others if the reports proved to be inaccurate.

When challenged three days before the election to justify the claim that children were thrown overboard, the Prime Minister produced an Office of National Assessments report to silence his critics. Once again, this contained a crumb of credibility — the report was nothing more than a rehashing of inaccurate government claims. ONA had even warned the Prime Minister's office that the report was hollow, but the people were never told. The government's entire children-overboard claim was in reality based on the same principles used by *People* magazine to justify stories about the infidelities of Hollywood stars. The Prime Minister later employed the same principle when he justified sending Australian forces to Iraq, using fabricated and already discredited reports that Iraq had attempted to buy fissionable materials from Niger.

Second, the government released photographs purporting to show that parents had in fact thrown their children overboard. It quickly became apparent the photographs (which anyway proved only that some children were *in* the water, not that they had been *thrown* in) were not of the incident the government claimed them to be, but were from a completely separate occurrence. The Senate report into the incident shows that government representatives knew before the release of the photographs that there were doubts about whether they were connected to the supposed children-overboard event, but only doubts. Again, the government had the crumb of credibility it needed, and it maintained the fiction until after election day by refusing to correct the record, even though it knew the photographs were not what they were purported to be.[9]

Third, when pressured about whether he knew that the children had, in fact, not been thrown overboard and that the photographs were not about that incident, the Prime Minister and members of the government fell back on another crumb of credibility — the claim that at no stage were they *officially* informed *in writing* that what they had said was misleading. It was also denied that the matter had been raised in telephone conversations, which can be proved to have happened by looking at telephone records. We will never know, however, what was said in private. The government did not have truth on its side, only 'deniability'. In *Nineteen Eighty-Four*, inconvenient published evidence was destroyed by the Ministry of Truth by throwing it down the 'memory hole' to be consumed by fire. In 2001, a sophisticated new government media machine stopped the evidence being recorded in the first place.

Fourth, in the last week of the federal election campaign, the government released a video that it had earlier claimed, without foundation, showed parents throwing their children overboard from the SIEV 4. Again, the video showed nothing of the kind. The most likely explanation for its public release — remembering that it had up until then been withheld from the public for security reasons — is political calculation. By the last week of the campaign, journalists were picking up rumblings about increasing desperation in the Liberal Party campaign. Labor's own polling showed it having edged ahead in the key marginal seats; and, while there is a wide margin of error in these figures, whatever the reality, there was a sense that Labor was storming home to an improbable victory. The release of the video was set up to take the election campaign back to the government's agenda of stopping asylum-seekers coming to Australia. The video was controversial and sensational. Although it failed to show parents throwing their children overboard, the truth didn't matter by that stage. Like the audience in Winston Smith's 'war flicks', all the electorate could see through the grainy images on the video were people whose very act of coming here posed a threat — the sort of people who would throw their children into the sea. All other issues were knocked off the front page and crowded out of the TV and radio news, and the rest is history.

An event was manufactured. Lies were told. Tracks were covered. Nothing could be proved. The 'two minute's hate' did its political job. Rarely outside the eastern-bloc countries of the communist era has there been a better example of the party's slogan in *Nineteen Eighty-Four* that 'Who controls the past controls the future. Who controls the present controls the past.'

The Howard government's behaviour during the 2001 federal election is a symptom of a deepening crisis in our political system: a decline in respect for the truth. In the past, although our political battles were hard fought, there was general agreement on the facts being debated. Today that has changed. The strategy of the Howard government since the arrival of the Tampa and the children-overboard affair has been to invent episodes that never occurred, refuse to acknowledge events that did, and pollute the historical record through a radical scepticism about whether any event that can possibly be contested happened at all. The *Minority Report of the Senate Select Committee on a Certain Maritime Incident* is a perfect display of this technique of refusing to accept that what happened actually happened. It was a deliberate 'truth-spoiling' operation which was, ironically, based on an (erroneous) appeal to Orwell — to whom the authors refer, mysteriously and without citation, to attack the use of evidence in the Majority Report.[10]

Orwell recognised that without basic agreement about the facts there can be no serious discussion of issues. The powerless can be traduced for something they didn't do, and the powerful can get away with political murder. Political murder is once again respectably clothed in phrases of evasion and downright lies. But governments can only get away with such behaviour if the people and, especially, journalists let them. Let's look at the state of political commentary in Australia today. Have some political commentators made this debasement of our politics easier?

Politics and the Australian language

How did the Howard government get away with the children-overboard scandal and the drowning of innocent people? Part of the answer lies in the willingness of the Australian people to be deceived over this particular issue. One talkback caller summed up the feelings of many, remarking that if the asylum-seekers hadn't tried to enter Australia, the government wouldn't have been forced to lie to us. So strong was the public's demand that action be taken to stop asylum-seekers coming to Australia that they saw the government's willingness to lie to them as a sign of its seriousness to fulfil their wishes.

Another explanation lies in the deliberate political misuse of language to envelop the issue in a fog of deception. Hardly a newspaper is published these days without a letter-writer, columnist, or editorial leader-writer using the term 'Orwellian' to describe political language that is deliberately elastic, ambiguous, or contradictory, designed to conceal the real nature of the sometimes monstrous behaviour it condones. All parties and governments use 'Orwellian' language, and it is nothing new. My first experience of the term as a school student was the naming of the MX missile 'the Peacemaker' by the Reagan administration. Today it manifests itself in terms such as 'Operation Iraqi Freedom', used by the Fox news network for their coverage of the Iraq War. Since the arrival of the Tampa, the term has become a commonplace for its aptness in describing the intent behind the language used by the Howard government to describe asylum-seekers. Here, for instance, is a newspaper letter-writer on the use by the Immigration Minister, Philip Ruddock, of the term 'unlawful non-citizens':

> This is language designed to discourage compassion, to exorcise empathy from the Australian public, to replace "the fair go" with fear and loathing. Language that seeks to demean us. To harden our hearts. The language is reminding us that those we once knew as "boatpeople" and "refugees" fleeing a totalitarian regime are simple criminals. The Orwellian phrase leaves no doubt that they can barely claim a right to exist, let alone be treated according to our obligations under international treaty.[11]

As many admirers of Orwell, including Bob Ellis and Robert Manne, have argued, numerous 'Orwellian' terms such as 'queue jumpers', 'detention centres', 'border protection', 'Pacific Solution', 'Suspected Illegal Entry Vessel', and the like have entered our language since the arrival of the Tampa. Children imprisoned behind barbed wire have been called 'it'; others who have sewn their lips together have been accused of 'inappropriate behaviour'; and even the prudent act of putting on a lifejacket while on the high seas in a leaky boat has been referred to as 'intimidation'. Manne has argued that, 'In writing about politics and the English language, Orwell might have had Philip Ruddock in mind ... By teaching Australians to think and speak like this, the minister has gradually helped to reconcile a goodly part of the nation to the unspeakable cruelties enacted daily' in the name of his asylum-seeker policy. In May 2003, wags at the Media, Entertainment and Arts Alliance even honoured minister Ruddock with the inaugural Orwell Award for obstructing press freedom.[12]

Because of the ubiquity of the expression 'Orwellian', these points will be familiar to most readers. But by employing Orwell's insight into the political misuse of language, Australian writers have hit on something deeper. Even before the arrival of the Tampa, a number of commentators had begun to notice the use of new words to help engineer a change in the nation's previously egalitarian culture.

In a meditation on Orwell's essay 'Politics and the English Language', Don Watson reminds us that, to some extent, this happens under all political parties and in all eras. For instance, according to Watson, the language of the 1980s — 'the language of the new productivity' — full of terms such as 'commitment', 'enhancement', and 'community' acted as 'an anaesthetic' delivered by politicians under the sway of economics to attune us to the new economic realities.[13] (Perhaps the inability of so many contemporary centre-left policy-makers to think politically and engage the public is caused by their continuing rhetorical imprisonment by this corporatist language. They have to learn to let it go.) A similar but even more far-reaching transformation of the national culture is underway under the Howard government, making us meaner and narrower minded.

Many have noticed that our prime minister is 'a master of the political art of deceiving without lying'.[14] He is also the master of conveying subtle meaning — getting us to accept fundamental change without confronting the full implications of what we are doing. Instead of reconciliation, we now have 'practical reconciliation' — a negation of the original intent of reconciliation, which was to promote mutual understanding. Instead of an apology to our indigenous peoples, we now have 'regret', which evades the whole idea of accepting responsibility. Instead of higher university fees, we have 'increased opportunities for individuals to invest in their education'. Policies designed to limit the bulk billing of medical services are called 'A Fairer Medicare'. And principled dissenters are labelled 'undemocratic elites' — as if the essence of democracy is compliance.

The commentator Ramona Koval has pointed out that Orwell would have recognised what was going on, by pointing to one of his more trenchant observations: 'When there is a gap between one's real and one's declared aims, one turns, as it were, instinctively to long words and exhausted idioms, like a cuttlefish squirting out ink.' Without the majority of Australian people noticing, she explains, a stunning rhetorical coup has been carried out: the bigotry that underpinned Hansonism has found a place in the insincere language and callous policies of the ruling party.[15] Throw a frog into a pot of boiling water and it will jump straight out. But if you take a more deceptive approach and boil the pot slowly, the frog will not notice before it is too late, and it will be cooked. This is what has happened to Australia's morality under John Howard. How did it occur?

John Howard has had spectacular success in changing the nation's collective morality without us realising, partly because of the structural inability of our news services to engage the public in wider debate about what is happening to our society. Most people get their political news from television, but the current format of TV news bulletins works against detailed discussion of key issues. Most nightly TV bulletins have a similar format. Federal politics is usually allocated a slot of no more than two to three minutes — which means that, however many newsworthy stories about federal politics are around on a given day, only one story, sometimes two, is usually covered. Unless there's a war on, sport gets more time than federal politics. This is a peculiarly Australian phenomenon; it does not happen on the BBC, for instance. The creeping phenomenon of 'celebrity journalism' means that federal news stories often resemble cheeky editorials; in any case, time constraints mean there's little possibility of getting beyond the day-to-day 'insider' political dramas of 'who's up and who's down', which sometimes resembles racetrack reporting more than a serious discussion of the issues that are being fought out by our elected representatives.

There are notable exceptions, such as the ABC's *7.30 Report* and *Lateline*, SBS's *Dateline*, and Nine's *Sunday*, but all have relatively low ratings and can't hope to balance the shallow coverage provided by prime-time commercial news bulletins and current affairs shows. While there is at least a fair degree of choice for viewers, the effect generally is to encourage a shallow understanding of our political system and a populist contempt for politicians.

The forum in which there should be serious and in-depth discussion of political issues is the newspaper opinion pages.

Like talkback radio hosts, the 'op ed' writers have an enormous influence on the formation of elite and public opinion on economic, social, and political events. They shape how many people interpret the news. In focus-group tests, the opinions of the lead commentators are frequently repeated by participants. Total objectivity is impossible in the opinion pages but, in the interests of democracy, there should at least be balance. However, in recent years the opinion pages have become increasingly dominated by biased commentators who see it as their duty to shield their favoured politicians and promote their political causes while stabbing at their opponents from close range. These commentators exist on all sides, but today are overwhelmingly on the side of the conservatives, supporting the Prime Minister's culture crusade. Orwellian language is their forte, and Orwell would immediately have recognised their vices.

Orwell's thoughts on the decline of the English language are the most popularly known part of his work, but they are merely the surface expression of a set of ideas that run deep through his thought and his character. Understanding this is crucial to grasping the full significance of the abuse of our language.

An objection to imprecise and cowardly political language was embedded in Orwell's personality and sense of aesthetics. To Orwell, such political language was a symptom of the general prefabrication of life that had been underway since the end of the First World War. Orwell's aesthetic preferences were very Edwardian, as anyone who reads his wistful 1939 novel about return to his childhood home, *Coming up for Air*, will discover. Here, for instance, is a passage from that novel describing the sensation of biting into a sausage bought by the main character, George Bowling, at the 1930s equivalent of McDonalds:

> It gave me the feeling that I'd bitten into the modern world and discovered what it was really made of. That's the way things are going nowadays. Everything slick and streamlined, everything made out of something else. Celluloid, rubber, chromium-steel everywhere, arc lamps blazing all night, glass roofs over your head, radios all playing the same tune, no vegetation left, everything cemented over, mock-turtles grazing under the neutral fruit-trees. But when you come down to brass tacks and get your teeth into something solid, a sausage for instance, that's what you get. Rotten fish in rubber skin. Bombs of filth bursting inside your mouth.[16]

Orwell loved the unspoiled English countryside, real ale, properly brewed tea, and hand-crafted furniture in the same way that he liked a beautifully balanced English sentence. You can read about it in his delightful wartime columns in *Tribune.* His love of the English language, which we can read in his magnificent essays on Dickens, Swift, and Kipling, was an expression of his deep English patriotism, which sent him into dreamy soliloquies about 'old maids biking to Holy Communion through the mists of autumn mornings'.[17]

Orwell's aesthetic as well as political revulsion at the decline of the English language was expressed through one of his greatest fictional creations, 'newspeak' — an 'Ikea' language, which was designed to make the expression of political dissent impossible. 'Newspeak' was partly satire, but it had a serious side — Orwell saw it as the logical final development of the tendency he recognised much earlier of contemporary language towards an imprecision that justified political barbarism. In the year 1984, in the novel *Nineteen Eighty-Four*, newspeak was still only in its early stages of development, but English as a tool for the expression of individual belief, complex human emotions, and freedom had already been largely destroyed. Instead of thinking deeply about what they said, the characters in *Nineteen Eighty-Four* spoke in ugly political sound bites that expressed the orthodoxy of 'the Party'. Orwell called it 'duckspeak'. Here's his description of it in a memorable scene when Winston Smith overhears a workmate's conversation in the Ministry of Truth canteen:

> What was slightly horrible, was that from the stream of sound that poured out of his mouth it was almost impossible to distinguish a single word. Just once Winston caught a phrase — 'complete and final elimination of Goldsteinism' — jerked out very rapidly and, as it seemed, all in one piece, like a line of type cast solid. For the rest it was just a noise, a quack-quack-quacking. And yet, though you could not actually hear what the man was saying, you could not be in any doubt about its nature. He might be denouncing Goldstein and demanding sterner measures against thought-criminals and saboteurs, he might be fulminating against the atrocities of the Eurasian army, he might be praising Big Brother or the heroes on the Malabar front — it made no difference. Whatever it was, you could be certain that

> every word of it was pure orthodoxy, pure Ingsoc. As he watched the eyeless face with the jaw moving rapidly up and down, Winston had a curious feeling that this was not a real human being but some kind of dummy. It was not the man's brain that was speaking, it was his larynx.[18]

Have you ever had this same feeling reading the opinion pages of our newspapers? Everyone, from high school students to letter writers and journalists, understands the concept of newspeak, but it is this less obvious 'duckspeak' that has infected much of Australia's contemporary political commentary. The biggest offenders are a group of right-wing commentators whose opinions are highly influential in our political debate. Let's look at some representative examples from some of the worst offenders.

P.P. McGuinness:

> Abbott might have done better to have avoided the doggerel of the bush priest, however, because the worst whingers, the urban elites, are a product of a quite different syndrome — the baby-boomer mindset. This, the most spoiled generation in world history, took control, as they thought, of the political and social system through a series of babyish tantrums in the 60's and 70's. Necessarily, they are now the real controllers of the system — the top bureaucrats, top businessmen, top managers, lawyers and judges, school principals, politicians and editors. And while they fear they might be responsible for a good deal of the social chaos

> we see around us, they do not want to admit it (especially those baby-boomer feminists who look at the disasters wrought by the breakdown of the nuclear family). So they resort to complaining about and denouncing whatever scapegoat is on offer for the day. Thus all the problems of Aborigines are not their fault, though they have been formulating policy for 30 years, but of their forebears. Ill-health is the fault of the cigarette companies, not their own youthful excesses. The degeneration of the education system is not because they are running it, but due to "economic rationalism" ... Underlying all these fears and dissatisfactions is the fear of looming retirement.

Andrew Bolt:

> [Bob] Brown says he isn't blaming Howard for Bali, but a blind fool can see his leering wink. On it goes. A conga line of hissing and spitting academics and activists has partied through the letters pages of the stridently Left-wing Fairfax newspapers to blame Howard for these appalling deaths. It is sick. It is sinister. And it is utterly wrong. In fact — and here is the irony — this campaign to blame Howard is waged by the very people *who more than most may have provoked the terrorists responsible for the Bali barbarity.* (Bolt's own emphasis.)

Piers Akerman:

> The Senate Inquiry into a certain maritime incident which concluded on July 30 was nothing more than a political picnic

> staged by a disgruntled Opposition with the assistance of a handful of conspiratorial malcontents of dubious intellectual credentials.'
>
> There is something intrinsically pathetic about the contrived outrage expressed by the opposition, neighbouring nations and the shrill voices of the ABC at Prime Minister Howard's responsible response to the threat of international terrorism.[19]

One will find similar theories in the columns of others such as Imre Salusinszky, Janet Albrechtson, Les Carlyon, and Christopher Pearson. Note the consistent ideological theme — expressed in tired, tabloid sound bites — that, since the 1960s and 1970s, society has been captured by a 'shrill-voiced', 'baby boomer', 'new class elite', 'conga line of hissing and spitting' teachers, academics, lawyers, feminists, social workers and, especially, 'stridently left-wing' ABC and Fairfax press journalists of 'dubious intellectual credentials', who are driven by the fear of their impending retirement and who are to blame for everything from 'the breakdown of the nuclear family' to the Bali bombing. These extracts aren't just evidence-free generalisations that would have trouble passing a year-twelve English clear-thinking test; they're examples of where the assembling of pre-packaged political phrases has been substituted for evidence and argument. Orthodoxy has replaced thought. If you lean down closer to the page you can hear the 'quack-quack-quacking'.

In our democracy, commentators are meant to be like cricket umpires, exercising judgements on behalf of citizens not parties

But, too often, Australian opinion columnists resemble the figure every gnarled old batsman has encountered — the umpire who once played for the opposing side who enthusiastically joins in with the bowler's appeal before giving you out. While many left-wing commentators have extreme political views, none advocate consistently in favour of Labor as many right-wing commentators consistently do in favour of the Liberal Party.

Ironically, conservative commentators often claim to be fans of Orwell. While their arguments may owe something to Orwell's distrust of intellectuals and bureaucrats, they represent at best an ossification of Orwell's ideas, reduced to a cliché, removed from their historical context, their anger robbed of Orwell's much remarked-upon generosity. Rather than being disciples of Orwell, they represent everything he detested. In *Nineteen Eighty-Four*, language is so devoid of original thought that it is even written by machines. Advances in word-processing technology open interesting new possibilities: an infinite number of monkeys given an infinite number of typewriters probably couldn't write *Hamlet*, but it can't be beyond the bounds of possibility for a piece of software pre-programmed with the Liberal Party's playbook to reproduce the thoughts of some of Australia's right-wing commentators.

What Orwell really disliked about the sausage-machine language that dominates too much political debate is that it makes acts of barbarity easier to justify. In his great essay from 1946, 'Politics and the English Language' (the bible of every serious political writer), Orwell lists five rules for good writing:

> (i) Never use a metaphor, simile or other figure of speech which you are used to seeing in print.
> (ii) Never use a long word where a short one will do.
> (iii) If it is possible to cut a word out, always cut it out.
> (iv) Never use the passive where you can use the active.
> (v) Never use a foreign phrase, a scientific word or a jargon word if you can think of an everyday English equivalent.

Louis Menand has pointed out that there's nothing particularly original about these rules. They could be found, for instance, in Fowler's *Modern English Usage*, which was in its fourth edition when Orwell wrote his essay.[20] The most important and original rule, however, is the sixth and last:

> (vi) 'Break any of these rules sooner than say anything outright barbarous.'[21]

Obviously, one of the chief types of barbaric thought to Orwell was totalitarianism, but he also greatly disliked nationalism. Orwell was a proud patriot. He saw *patriotism* as primarily a defensive value, concerned with celebrating culture and place, but he believed that *nationalism* was too easily abused for base ends. Like totalitarianism, nationalism was connected to power worship. Both produced passions that overwhelmed the senses and led people to deny that what is true is true. For the nationalist, 'actions are held to be good or bad, not on their own merits but according to who does them, and there is no kind of outrage — torture, the use of hostages, forced labour, mass deportations ... — which does not change its moral colour when committed by 'our' side.' Inconvenient facts are forgotten and others are reinterpreted to fit 'our side's' needs. 'A known fact may be so unbearable that it is habitually pushed aside and not allowed to enter into logical processes, or on the other hand it may enter into every calculation and yet never be admitted as a fact, even in one's own mind ... Loyalty is involved, and so pity ceases to function.'[22]

It is worth, at this point, returning to Orwell's criticism of Auden's poem *Spain* and its phrase 'the necessary murder':

> Mr Auden's brand of amoralism is only possible if you are the kind of person who is always somewhere else when the trigger is pulled. So much left-wing thought is a kind of playing with fire by people who don't even know that fire is hot. The warmongering to which the English intelligentsia gave themselves up in the period 1935–9 was largely based on a sense of personal immunity. The attitude is very different in France where the military service is hard to dodge and even literary men know the weight of a pack'[23]

The most bellicose and nationalistic Australian writers of today fit Orwell's description perfectly, except that today they're on the right, not the left. Many conservative commentators have engaged in unrelenting and sometimes viciously personal attacks on the patriotism and motivations of the Australian peace movement during the recent war in Iraq, even though some had been opponents of Australia's involvement in the

Vietnam War. Bellicosity and the character assassination of peace activists is a little hard to take from men who, when they were young enough to know the weight of a pack, weren't prepared to fight for their country against communist totalitarianism. George Orwell supported some wars and opposed others, but he at least had the courage to fight for democracy before denouncing those who wouldn't.

The prevention of Australian literature

One of the ugliest and saddest aspects of culture-war politics is the way culture warriors reduce every cultural product to one dimension only — politics. There's no room for balanced aesthetic judgements, only political ones, and no room either for the generosity and respect for artistic creation that characterises mature cultural debate. This is seriously corroding the quality of political and cultural discussion in Australia. It is a deterioration that Orwell was awake to in his own day.

Orwell greatly disliked the politicisation of every aspect of life. Everything, he said, did not have to have a 'class angle' — a crucial feature of his thought which, as we have seen in the previous chapter, was recognised by Pierre Ryckmans. This is best seen in Orwell's essay 'Benefit of Clergy', which is a review of the autobiography of Salvador Dali. This essay is notable not just for its comments on the relationship between politics and aesthetics, but also its observation that 'autobiography is only to be trusted when it reveals something disgraceful'. By this measure, Dali's was a very good autobiography indeed. It revealed his necrophilia, his homicidal impulses, and his refusal to take sides against fascism. While Orwell found Dali revolting and cowardly, he did not find this a good reason to suppress his art or overlook his artistic talent. Orwell wrote that there were two general views on the relationship between culture and politics: 'Kulturbolschevismus' and 'Art for Art's sake'. Proponents of the former believed that it is not possible to be a good artist and be politically incorrect, while those who held the second viewpoint were claiming a kind of 'benefit of clergy'. Just as clergymen in the middle ages were able to claim exemption from the criminal law because they were literate, some believed artists should be exempted from the moral laws that bind ordinary people just because they can paint or write or otherwise create. Both arguments, Orwell believed, are wrong:

> One ought to be able to hold in one's head simultaneously the two facts that Dali is a good draughtsman and a disgusting human being. The one does not invalidate or, in a sense, affect the other. The first thing we demand of a wall is that it shall stand up. If it stands up, it is a good wall, and the question of what purpose it serves is separable from that. And yet even the best wall in the world deserves to be pulled down if it surrounds a concentration camp. In the same way it should be possible to say, 'This is a good book or a good picture, and it ought to be burned by the public hangman.' Unless one can say that, at least in imagination, one is shrinking the implications of the fact that an artist is also a citizen and a human being.[24]

Orwell's position is that, while works of art should be criticised for their political implications, we have to be careful that we don't overdo it and make politics art's only measure. We must keep a sense of proportion. Unfortunately, this sense of proportion is lacking among some of Australia's right-wing tabloid commentators. Films, books, radio programs, art exhibitions, academic texts — any cultural statement, in fact — that is at odds with their brand of conservatism is subjected to a political and sometimes viciously personal review, usually with no positive acknowledgement, however grudging, of its artistic qualities. There are, of course, no arrests or public recantations in these culture wars, such as those forced on an Oscar Wilde or Dimitri Shostakovich. There's just a relentless campaign of denigration and brutal character assassination by people who should know better.

P.P. McGuinness says, for instance, of the *Oxford Companion to Australian History* only that it 'is a kind of compendium of every wild allegation advanced for political or other purposes against earlier generations of white historians.'[25] Does the book — edited by a committee of some of the most eminent historians in the nation and drawing upon peer-reviewed work from dozens of university history departments from across the country — have any academic merit? It appears not, if part of it contradicts the political views of the editor of *Quadrant.*

A favourite recent target of the tabloid commentators — in concert with conservative politicians — is filmmaker Philip Noyce, maker of *Rabbit-Proof Fence* and *The Quiet American.* The commentators' response to these films was utterly predictable, to the extent of creating a suspicion that it was a coordinated hit. Within days of its release, *Rabbit-Proof Fence* was howled down by right-wing politicians as well as commentators as 'elite propaganda'. Liberal Party MP Peter Slipper objected that the poster promoting the film portrayed Australia in a bad light, hinting at its author's lack of patriotic sentiment. He even asked the film promoters for an apology — which the Liberal/National Party government of John Howard pointedly refused the stolen generations themselves. Right-wing senator Eric Abetz attacked the film for claiming there was ever such a thing as the 'stolen generations'. Multicultural Affairs Minister Gary Hardgrave supported Abetz.[26] But the worst 'culture bolsheviks' were Piers Akerman and Andrew Bolt. Both used their columns to claim that the filmmaker Phillip Noyce had changed several key facts about the story on which the film was based in order to enhance its political point. Bolt went even further, writing that Noyce had in fact 'stolen' one the Aboriginal children who starred in the film.[27] This type of viciousness should have no place in our cultural discussions; but, sadly, it is on a par with other similar pieces of cheap demagoguery.

The Quiet American faced a similar storm to *Rabbit-Proof Fence*. Gerard Henderson (a former chief of staff to Prime Minister John Howard) used his column to attack the Graham Greene novel on which the film was based as an anti-American text, written by a communist fellow traveller, and to accuse film-maker Noyce of making the film even more anti-American than Greene's book. There was no educated appraisal of its merit as a piece of cinematography, despite the critical acclaim given to the performance of Michael Caine.[28]

There is, of course, nothing wrong with political commentators voicing opinions on the political implications of art. But today in Australia the fashion has become so widespread that it's starting to become shallow, demagogic, and predictable, and to poison our cultural debates. Instead of a mature national conversation about our values and beliefs, informed by a deep understanding of culture and aesthetics, we're getting a shouting match that is ugly and demeaning. Orwell, short of a quid at the start of the Second World War, tried his hand at film reviews but was self aware enough to know that it wasn't his calling and soon gave it up. It's an enormous pity that so many right-wing Australian political commentators — with the notable exception of Peter Coleman on a good day — lack a level of cultural understanding that would add more subtlety and depth to their reporting of issues that are not strictly political. Compare the relentlessly ideological and one-dimensional amateurism of Bolt and Henderson with some excerpts from this review of *Rabbit-Proof Fence* by *The Australian*'s film reviewer, Evan Williams. I quote it at some length to give readers a feel for the depth of cinematographic and balanced political understanding that *is* possible, but which we just don't get from our right-wing commentators:

> This is the first film about the stolen generations and it's important in the best sense of the word. That doesn't mean that it's a very good film, still less a complete success. I wish it were. But it carries an overwhelming sense of conviction. And what

> makes much of it compelling is its lack of self-important flourishes. The story is slight, the direction understated, the cast largely untried. In one respect it reminded me of *Schindler's List*. At the end of that film, Spielberg tacked on a little epilogue in which the characters appeared as themselves, old and worn, but somehow recognisable. Noyce uses the same device. Molly and Daisy, two of the girls in the story, are seen at the end as elderly women. And after all they have endured the effect is oddly comforting. Here, it seems, is proof of their survival, proof that their story is real, proof, if you like, that their spirit lives on.
>
> At the risk of being misunderstood, I should say that I still find the story difficult to believe. It's not that I doubt anyone's good faith ... It's an amazing tale, though sceptics may prefer to see it as a fabric of childhood memories, embellished by repeated embroidering. But even if it were wholly invented it would have the power to stir us: *Rabbit-Proof Fence* has been made with such transparent humanity and idealism it scarcely seems to matter whether the story is true or not.'[29]

Williams thinks the film a partial failure, and he clearly doubts its strict factualness in parts. But film is Williams' *metier*, and the result is a critical but generous and multidimensional understanding, rather than the ideologically motivated and radically sceptical thuggery that appears all too often on the opinion pages, and leaves us with the feeling that we're being intellectually short changed.

As we have seen, Orwell's literary reviews did take account of the political views of writers and other artists; in fact, his reviews were *very* political. However, he recognised that political judgements were only one aspect of a reviewer's task; otherwise, literature might as well be written by political parties and pre-programmed machines (as it was in his novel *Nineteen Eighty-Four*). Clive James has written that Orwell wrote his reviews not just as a political commentator, but as 'a superb literary critic himself' and 'the first person to read on Swift, on Dickens and on Gissing' who, had he lived to a full term, 'might have gone on to become the greatest modern literary critic in the language'. As James points out, Orwell died before completing a planned essay on Evelyn Waugh. Had he completed it, 'it would have been the best thing on the subject, the essay that really opens up Waugh's corrosively snobbish view of life without violating his creative achievement.'[30] That type of generous criticism, and not the constriction and ferocity we get from our political writers, is what Australia sorely needs more of today.

Perhaps we'd all be better off if our art was subjected to a little less neo-conservative amateur sociology and a little more balanced, informed criticism . Our cultural debates badly need a calmer tone that understands the importance of art and Orwell's principle that not everything has to have a political angle. There's too much politically driven extremism in our public debates. We need some of Orwell's passion for reason that led him to always put the truth before dogma. Ironically, by reducing everything to the single dimension of politics, our tabloid commentators are playing the same game as the 'second-rate', 'postmodernist' 'cultural commissars' in our universities and the Fairfax press whom they relentlessly attack. The tactic used is always the same: denouncing as unpatriotic and undemocratic anyone whose ideas on key issues are at odds with the Howard-supporting majority, especially those in receipt of public moneys. Andrew Bolt is the master of this device: higher-education institutions are called 'Looney Unis' and 'the Footscray Kremlin' for running courses Bolt disagrees with; writers, historians, and artists in receipt of Australia Council grants are denounced as unpatriotic propagandists; and the Australian Greens are likened to the Nazi Party.[31]

Why have right-wing commentators chosen to take their stand on issues such as Aboriginal affairs, the US alliance, universities, and the arts? The first answer is, of course, sheer populism. There will always be a receptive audience for yellow journalism, and the more provocative the better. The second answer involves politics. I've no doubt that right-wing commentators have sincerely held beliefs on these issues, but their writings wittingly or unwittingly play a vital part in a wider neo-conservative strategy of using race and patriotism to drive a wedge between blue-collar voters and centre-left parties such as Labor, the Australian Democrats, and the Greens — as I have argued above, in relation to the Tampa episode. By getting people to focus on cultural issues, conservatives try to distract them from far more important economic issues that involve their real interests, such as the state of our public schools and hospitals, the erosion of workplace rights and job security, and the steady transfer of wealth to the rich.

The hints are all there in the first of John Howard's 'headland' speeches from 1995, where he spelt out an early draft of the argument behind his subtle slogan 'for all of us', which has provided the underlying theme for the attacks on indigenous Australians and asylum-seekers of his government ever since. There are no less that fifteen references to supporters of Paul Keating as a 'bureaucracy of the new class', 'self-appointed cultural dieticians', 'puppets of special interests', and 'the noisy, self-interested clamour of powerful vested interests with scant regard for the national interest'.

The triumph of the new Australian orthodoxy

In 'The Prevention of Literature', where Orwell develops his criticisms of political writing further, he writes that, 'wherever there is an enforced political orthodoxy ... good writing stops ... To write in plain, vigorous language one has to think fearlessly, and if one thinks fearlessly one cannot be politically orthodox.'[32] The reason the writing of Australia's right-wing commentators is so appalling is that it has finally become the new orthodoxy. Our commentators like to pretend that they're being brave in questioning 'politically correct' norms like reconciliation, support for the United Nations, or opposition to the war in Iraq. But, while some of what they say may have offended sensibilities in 1995, today it's mainstream. You can sense it in their new triumphal tone. Here are a few brief examples:

Les Murray (*The Australian*, 1 January 2003):

> In 2002, as in every year since the defeat of the republic

> referendum in 1999, the atmosphere in Australia has grown a little less totalitarian.

Christopher Pearson (*The Australian*, 18 January 2003):

> things are less like they were in the 1980s and '90s than anyone could imagine at the time ... The wheels are wobbling off the triumphal chariot of progressivism and the cultural avant-garde, which once seemed unstoppable. Advocates of socially conservative values are losing the habitually beleaguered look.

Peter Ryan (*The Australian*, 10 January 2003):

> the minority rule of trendoid ratbaggery is ending, and we are returning our attention to less exciting matters, such as national survival in an envious and hostile region, and to the everyday sort of Australia that most people truly want ... This has not been done by the unaided effort of John Winston Howard, yet somehow one can't imagine it happening without him ... After years of venomous bias, the media are now changing their tone. Even journalists can see that Howard's political ascendancy is total ... Fifty years from now, when impartial history can be written, and the archives can be unlocked, the two decades straddling the millennium will be known as the Age of Howard.

Note the statement that 'Howard's political ascendancy is total'. Winning this culture war has been a remorseless and well-co-ordinated campaign by the neo-conservative backers of John Howard. But win they have. And Howard hasn't just been a follower; from the very start, he has been one of its leaders, pushing his views subtly and sometimes unsubtly on talkback radio, in public lectures, and in neo-conservative magazines such as *Quadrant*. In 1994, for instance, he lamented that Liberals in Australia had failed to counter the tendency of historians and commentators to identify Labor with the positive historical and cultural features of the nation:

> In fighting the battles of history with the Labor Party, the Liberals must remember George Orwell's proposition: 'Who controls the past, controls the future. Who controls the present controls the past.'
>
> There are still far too few Liberals who fully comprehend just how committed Paul Keating and many in the Labor Party are to the quite ruthless use of history — or more particularly their version of it — as a political weapon. Not only do they wish to reinterpret Australian history to promote their contemporary political objectives, but they also wish to marginalise the contribution of the conservative-liberal side of Australian politics and entrench the Labor Party as the only true product of Australia's political soil. There are signs of increased Liberal willingness to join battle with the Labor Party over both history and ideas. This is a trend which must be enthusiastically encouraged.[33]

He has quoted Orwell to make a similar point on a number of occasions. Howard's use of Orwell here to argue for the contesting of history goes, ironically, against Orwell's intention.

Orwell wanted to warn against the political control of the truth, including the facts of the past, by unscrupulous politicians. Howard here unwittingly illustrates a problem Orwell was trying to highlight. And you can see the results in the smouldering ruins of Australia's cultural debate.

The (mis) appropriation of Orwell

Howard's own words show George Orwell's enormous influence on the new culture war that grips Australia. (It's perhaps no coincidence that two foot soldiers in this culture war and Orwell admireres — Gerard Henderson and Christopher Pearson — are former Howard speechwriters. While it's true that Henderson can be more unpredictable than Pearson, and differs with most neo-conservatives on issues such as multiculturalism, his views on many other cultural issues often coincide with those of Howard's neo-conservative backers, and he often gently chides his former boss for failure to prosecute his culture war more successfully.[34]) This influence rests on a highly conservative interpretation of Orwell's thought, the origins of which I discussed in chapter one. I believe that this is in large part a *mis*-interpretation, based on a highly selective reading of Orwell.-

The essence of the problem with the conservatives' misappropriation of Orwell can be seen in the work of Andrew Bolt. To put it most simply, Orwell was a man of the left. Asked by a reporter from *The Australian* to nominate his favourite journalist, Bolt has no hesitation in nominating George Orwell. Bolt believes that it is right-wing commentators such as him, who expose 'vastly overblown destructive myth(s)' such as the 'stolen generations', who represent the true spirit of Orwell — 'the lone voice speaking the truth while all around him a hegemony of media denial deprives the public of what it knows deep down to be true.'[35] If Bolt has hit on a truth about Orwell, it is only a partial truth. The lone voice of the contrarian, courageously stating the ugly truth, encapsulates part of Orwell's style, but not his beliefs. (In fact, many right-wing media commentators are not true 'contrarians' at all. Their aim isn't unpopularity but populism. Their target isn't the fearless lone-wolf citizen, but the G-spot of anger and resentment that lies in everyone's subconscious.) As Pierre Ryckmans demonstrated in his argument against the neo-conservative claiming of Orwell in the 1980s, the Orwell of Barcelona who fearlessly told the truth against the communist lie machine did so because he stood up for the poor and the downtrodden, not the political status quo.

It is difficult to imagine the Orwell who so vehemently opposed the communist gulag system and British imperialism — despite acknowledging that it was probably better than other imperialisms — being in favour of locking children behind razor wire in the middle of a hostile wilderness, coming down on the side of the Howard government over the stolen generations, or seeing the 'children overboard' affair as anything but an attempt to manufacture the truth in the name of political power. I will explore Orwell's political beliefs at length in the next chapter. I believe that, while Orwell would have exposed exaggerations and debunked lies surrounding these controversies, he would have made sure he kept on the side of the underdog. Bolt and his allies, by contrast, do not.

Conservatives are on stronger ground when they cite Orwell to criticise the absurdity and out-of-touch elitism of some of Australia's left-wing intellectuals. One can imagine Orwell, like Bolt, Akerman, and others, rolling his eyes over some of the excesses on Australian university campuses or ABC arts programs, for example. However, Orwell's attack on left-wing intellectuals was altogether different from that of the neo-conservative public intellectuals discussed in this chapter. Orwell had no time for many of his left-wing intellectual contemporaries, not because they professed to be left wing but because they *discredited* the socialist movement of his day. He lamented the fact that so many socialist thinkers were out of touch with the values and priorities of the ordinary citizen and potential socialist (meaning, for Orwell, left-wing British Labour) voters. Why, he asked, did ordinary people invariably associate socialism with people he called 'quacks'? By using their common sense, intellectuals, he thought, could help build a movement that could bind ordinary middle-class and working-class people to a practical but quite radical political platform.

This seems to me to be totally at odds with the journalistic priorities of Australia's neo-conservatives. Again, it's a case of them following Orwell's style but not his content. Our neo-conservatives set out to discredit left-wing intellectuals for the opposite reason to Orwell — to ridicule even mainstream left-wing ideas and undermine potential connections between the educated leadership of parties such as the Greens, the Democrats, and Labor and ordinary Australians.

The other major area where Australia's neo-conservatives 'claim' Orwell is in foreign policy. Orwell's authority has been invoked regularly since the September 11 attacks on the United States to argue the case that people on the left should be on the side of the United States in tackling international terrorism. The most prominent left thinker has been the US-based English intellectual Christopher Hitchens, whose books *Letters to a Young Contrarian* and *Orwell's Victory* show Orwell as Hitchens' consistent source of inspiration. Hitchens has broken with many on the left because he believes that the 'war on terrorism' is a war on 'fascism with an Islamic face' and, like the Spanish Civil War and the Second World War, the sort of war that someone like George Orwell, who passionately believed in democracy, would have supported. This line of argument has been taken up strongly by commentators such as Imre Salusinszky and Gerard Henderson, who have accused a number of left-wing Australian columnists — particularly *Arena* editor Guy Rundle, *Australian* columnist Philip Adams, and Radio National's Terry Lane — of being unpatriotic (although Salusinszky praised others, such as *Age* commentator Pamela Bone, for supporting the war on terrorism).

Henderson drew specifically on Orwell's famous 1945 essay, 'Notes on Nationalism', to explain why support for the coalition parties rose during the Iraq War when polls had shown a majority opposed the War before it started. Australians, he argued, were essentially 'patriotic', but not 'nationalistic'. While they rally around the flag when Australians are in harm's way, they do not support aggressive wars that seek to foist their values on others. Australia's left-wing intellectuals, Henderson implies, should do the same, but too often can be found supporting brutal nationalist regimes such as that of Saddam Hussein. This is a very Orwell-like position. Orwell believed that the inability of left-wing intellectuals to see patriotism as a virtue was one of the things that reduced their popular support. Whether this in itself is an argument for supporting the war in Iraq is another matter. As one letter-writer to the *Sydney Morning Herald* put it, many of those in the United States who argued for the war in Iraq did so precisely because they did want to assert US power and foist their system of government on the people of Iraq.

Rundle defended himself against charges of being unpatriotic by arguing that while Orwell was an English patriot, his position was more complex than that presented by Henderson. Rundle points out that, in the 1941 essay 'The Lion and the Unicorn', Orwell declared that he wanted not only to win the Second World War to defeat fascism — like Hitchens and the 'War on Terror' — but to turn it into a revolutionary war to advance the cause of socialism. Rundle also argues that the war may have brought out the strong anti-colonialist streak in Orwell, who would have been appalled that the lives of many thousands of innocent Iraqis would have been put at risk through the overwhelming use of US military might.

While Hitchens and others have a strong case that Orwell would have supported a war in favour of democracy and against 'Islamic fascists' such as the Al Qaeda and Jemaah Islamiyah networks, we can be less certain that he would have supported the Iraq War. He very well may have done so, but he may also have regarded it as another of the endless wars fought in former colonial countries that the Party in *Nineteen Eighty-Four* used to keep its population on a constant war footing. We will never know. We can be certain of one thing, however: the revelations that the evidence used by the US, British, and Australian administrations to justify the war was thin and, in parts, completely made up, would have led Orwell to warn us about the tendency of all governments to manufacture the truth to further their own power and ends.[36]

Getting inside the whale

To Orwell, most political writing of his day was bad. It was dominated by the left-wing and right-wing equivalents of today's tabloid commentators, armed with their ugly ideological and nationalistic biases and bolted-together language. Orwell asked the question: how can civilised values be defended against creeping barbarism and the undermining of democracy? For Orwell, the answer was not to swing to the left but to become more human. To write well, one had to make the difficult moral effort to struggle against ideological and nationalistic biases.[37] The good writer was a true rebel, not the follower of an ideology of rebellion.

This is the message of one of Orwell's best essays, 'Inside the Whale', in which he praised the provocative novel *Tropic of Cancer* by the American novelist Henry Miller, and criticised contemporary English writers for their submission to fashionable political beliefs. Miller's *Tropic of Cancer* had been banned from publication in Britain for its frank portrayal of amorality and bad language. It is still quite confronting. Surprisingly, Orwell — perhaps *the* political writer of the twentieth century — admired *Tropic of Cancer* precisely because it was a profoundly *un*political work in a profoundly political age. As Orwell writes, with Mussolini's troops marching into Abyssinia, and Hitler's concentration camps already bulging, an underworld tale of 'American deadbeats cadging drinks in the Latin Quarter' was unlikely material for an important statement about the contemporary world. Yet it was. Miller's novel was a product of the essential state of being that Orwell believed a writer must get him or herself into if they want to tell the truth and be taken seriously. He called this process 'getting inside the whale'. Here's what he meant (in a passage that reads like Miller and displays the significant influence that *The Tropic of Cancer* had on Orwell's pre-war books)[38]:

> There you are in the dark cushioned space that exactly fits you, with yards of blubber between yourself and reality, able to keep up an attitude of complete indifference no matter what happens. A storm that could sink all of the battleships in the world could hardly reach you as an echo. Even the whale's own movements would probably be imperceptible to you. He might be wallowing among the surface waves or shooting down into the blackness of the middle seas (mile deep according to Herman Melville), but you would never notice the difference. Short of being dead, it is the final, unsurpassable stage of irresponsibility. ... [T]here is no question that Miller himself is inside the whale. All the best and

> most characteristic passages are written from the angle of Jonah, a willing Jonah. Not that he is specially introverted — quite the contrary. In his case the whale happens to be transparent. Only he feels the impulse to alter or control the process that he is undergoing. He has performed the elemental Jonah act of allowing himself to be swallowed, remaining passive, accepting.[39]

While this at first sounds like a defence of quietism, for Orwell it is itself, paradoxically, a political act. Orwell believed that, by rejecting the ugly, clichéd ideologies of his age, Miller was reaffirming what it meant to be truly human; that he was writing about life as it really was, not as ideologies attempted to interpret and narrow it for us. Miller was 'the human voice among the bomb explosions, a friendly American voice "innocent of public spiritedness". No sermons, merely the subjective truth.'[40] Good writing required a struggle against ideological biases, and this could only be adequately undertaken by someone who set him or herself at an angle to society. It could only be written by a rebel.

Henry Miller certainly fitted the description of the rebel, although an apolitical one. He rejected all political commitment, and thought that any writer who, such as Orwell for instance, went to Spain to fight fascism was a fool. But Miller still appealed to Orwell. Orwell recognised that he and Miller shared something important — the stance of the true rebel. This part of Orwell's personality can be easily recognised in his eccentric appearance — dark, heavy-cotton shirt, worn tweed jacket, a severe haircut, and a hand-rolled cigarette permanently hanging out of the corner of the mouth (despite the worsening TB that was to kill him). This partly academic, partly proletarian appearance has been a model for millions of university students and writers ever since. Despite his Etonian background, Orwell himself got 'inside the whale' in *Down and Out in Paris and London*, *A Clergymans' Daughter*, *Keep the Aspidistra Flying*, and *The Road to Wigan Pier* — his descriptions of poverty and unemployment in the Great Depression.

Only by getting down into the boarding houses and dole queues with the victims of the Great Depression, living off bread and bacon and stewed tea, not pre-judging and trying to fit people into neat little ideological boxes, could Orwell write the only truth possible about the capitalism of his age — that the wealth of everyone from the middle classes up was built on the sweat, neglect, and poverty of the working classes. And only by doing this could he see the absurdity of the solutions proposed by the contemporary socialist movement. This is also how to understand the actions of the rebel character Winston Smith in *Nineteen Eighty-Four* Only when he had withdrawn to his alcove, away from the telescreen and the Party and its ideology, where he could be truly human, could he have the freedom to write the only truth possible to write about Oceania — 'Down with Big Brother'. Writers should not side with one ideology or another. Their goal had to be to reaffirm what it meant to be human and free in an age in which nasty little ideologies were contending for their souls. That was Orwell's mission. It needs to be ours, too.

CHAPTER THREE

The road to Fountain Gate

George Orwell had a lot of harsh things to say about some of his left-wing contemporaries. Here's one of his most oft-quoted passages. It's from an age when men generally wore long trousers, jackets, and ties:

> One sometimes gets the impression that the mere words 'Socialism' and 'Communism' draw towards them with magnetic force every fruit-juice drinker, nudist, sandal-wearer, sex-maniac, Quaker, 'Nature Cure' quack, pacifist, and feminist in England. One day this summer I was riding through Letchworth when the bus stopped and two dreadful-looking old men got on to it. They were both about sixty, both very short, pink, and chubby, and both hatless. One of them was obscenely bald, the other had long grey hair bobbed in the Lloyd George style. They were dressed in pistachio-coloured shirts and khaki shorts into which their huge bottoms were crammed so tightly that you could study every dimple. Their appearance created a mild stir of horror on top of the bus. The man next to me, a commercial traveller I should say, glanced at me, at them, and back again at me, and murmured 'Socialists', as who should say, 'Red Indians'.

> He was probably right — the I.L.P. [the Independent Labour Party] were holding their summer school at Letchworth.[1]

Many read comments such as this as proof that Orwell was not a true man of the left. They certainly show that he was a man of another age; modern feminists, for instance, would rightly be aghast. Arguments over this question, of how left wing or otherwise he was, have occupied some of the best critics of English literature and politics, from Raymond Williams to Salman Rushdie and Christopher Hitchens. Claims that Orwell was a man of the right are all too often made by angry old men who suspect that, had Orwell not died young but instead lived to old age, he would have turned out just like them — a reactionary, anti-socialist cold warrior. But such assertions can easily be dealt with by quoting Orwell's own words, written in 1946:

> Every line of serious work that I have written since 1936 has been written, directly or indirectly, *against* totalitarianism and *for* democratic socialism, as I understand it.[2]

Orwell's criticisms of his left-wing peers were not intended to undermine the socialist movement but, rather, to strengthen it. Socialism, as he saw it, was discredited not only by its association with totalitarianism, but also by the lack of real understanding between the educated middle-class left and working people. One of Orwell's recent biographers, Jeffrey Meyers, has made the crucial point that much of Orwell's life and writing was devoted to 'creating a human bridge between left-wing intellectuals and the most oppressed people in English society'.[3] He made it one of his life's goals to share and understand the experiences of ordinary people, and worked his way steadily from the bottom of society to somewhere in the middle: exploited colonial coolie (*Burmese Days*), homeless down-and-outer (*Down and Out in Paris and London*), seasonal labourer (*A Clergyman's Daughter*), unemployed miner (*The Road to Wigan Pier*), Spanish peasant (*Homage to Catalonia*), frustrated lower middle-class salesman (*Coming up for Air*), and penniless writer (*Keep the Aspidistra Flying*). These attempts to get 'inside the whale' had the goal of humanising the 'working classes' for the benefit of educated readers. His attacks on theoretical socialism were an attempt to make left-wing politics more practical and more appealing to ordinary people and the swinging voters of his day.

Here is one of the lessons that Orwell has for Australians today: the need for members of the tertiary-educated left to reconnect with the outer suburbs. Orwell's challenge to the left or the 'elites' to 'get real' is one we need to accept today. In this chapter, I aim to show that the answer to the swing to the right in Australian politics isn't for the 'elites' to swing further leftwards. Australia has perhaps never been more divided — by class, race, culture, and distance. One of the key reasons for this increased division is the dog-whistle wedge politics practised by the Howard government and the tabloid commentators who back it. But we are all responsible for this division, and we all need to make efforts to overcome these differences and to understand each other better.

All Australians are equal, but ...

Despite firing off arrows in all directions, Australia's tabloid commentators have hit the target only once — when they point out the divergence in political views between the tertiary-educated political class and the great mass of people who live in our suburbs and regions. This divergence has been obvious since at least the 1996 election when many, including Robert Manne, wrote of the emergence of two Australias — the one inside and the one outside the Sydney-Melbourne-Canberra triangle.

There is plenty of evidence to support this thesis, particularly in the pages of the Monash University journal *People and Place.* Robert Birrell and Virginia Rapson have reported how Melbourne and Sydney (or at least parts of those cities) are becoming more cosmopolitan than the rest of Australia, and that the birthplace of Australians is becoming a stronger indicator of voting intentions. On one telling issue — attitudes to refugees — Swinburne University researcher Katherine Betts has found distinct patterns of disagreement related to social class and geography. The central thesis of these researchers is that those most likely to support the Howard government's conservative stance on social questions are para-professionals, lower-level clerks, and people born in Australia.[4] But you don't need statistics to tell you this; in the morning, tune your radio to John Laws and Alan Jones, and then at night move across to 'Australia Talks Back' and Philip Adams' 'Late Night Live'.

Reports such as those by Birrell, Rapson, and Betts have been seized upon by right-wing commentators to support their attacks on what they see as the undemocratic 'new class elite'. But this divergence of opinion is only the surface manifestation of a wider problem: we are becoming a much more divided society in every sense. The same researchers have reported a social and economic divide that has widened alarmingly over the past decade. Unfortunately, you won't read about this in the columns of our tabloid commentators, who are usually careful to give only one dimension of this problem.

The full picture from *People and Place* and other sources is clear: Australia is seeing the emergence of two societies increasingly cut off from each other. One, based in wealthy, inner-city suburbs, with rising income and wealth — the sort of places where not only the educated left tend to live, but the millionaire commentators, too — dominates entry to our elite universities and occupations, and is characterised by affluence and access to opportunities that the poor can barely comprehend. And the other, trapped in declining suburbs and towns with houses they often can't afford to sell, has fewer opportunities for education and fewer chances of entry to well-paid professions. The former are having a smaller proportion of our children. The latter are having a larger proportion — often without the ability to provide for them adequately within the nest of a trusting and lasting family relationship. As a result, at least one in six of our children are being brought up in poverty.[5]

This is a social catastrophe waiting to happen. We're losing something important — the egalitarianism that is an essential part of the Australian way of life. This is the ugly reality about modern Australia that the Howard government's culture wars are deliberately designed to distract us from. Indeed, as Michael Pusey has pointed out, on many political and economic issues the views of working- and educated middle-class Australians are similar and against the status quo, but expressed in different ways.[6] This imperative to divide people dissatisfied with the status quo is the real reason that populism is replacing the national interest as the chief driver of government policy. And it's why the coalition behaves less like a national government responsible for all of us, and more like a narrow oligarchy that wants to help its supporters dodge their responsibilities to the rest of us.

Is this the type of fractured society we want? There is an alternative, but creating it won't be easy. Between these extremes of wealth and hardship is a sizeable, affluent working class — ordinary suburban Australians — sometimes referred to as 'middle Australia', who aren't overly politicised or welded to any party. They have become the contested electoral ground in an increasingly ruthless political battle. If some form of social democracy is to triumph again in Australia that can rebuild our egalitarian way of life, the left must learn to speak the language of these people again. As Orwell showed us, this takes a *moral* effort to get to know them, share their lives, and understand their concerns and motivations. Although it's only the first step, it's the hardest one to take. But if Orwell could take it, so can we.

The road to Fountain Gate

Bridging the divides between communities and classes is the subject of Orwell's second book, *The Road to Wigan Pier*, which is an extended piece of reportage drawn from his travels in the economically depressed north of England in 1936. The class divides in Britain at that time were, of course, much greater than those in Australia today, and where the economic divides today are just as great, television has given all sides at least some rudimentary understanding of how the other half lives. Living conditions in the north of England would have been almost unknown to an educated person from the relatively prosperous south. When *The Road to Wigan Pier* was first published, Philip Toynbee wrote that it 'reads like a report brought back by some humane anthropologist who has just returned from studying the conditions of an oppressed tribe in Borneo.'[7] Orwell's basic method is still useful today: look, listen, learn and, most of all, try to understand.

In the second half of *The Road to Wigan Pier*, Orwell explained just how difficult it was to get over class prejudices. Orwell described himself in his teen years as 'an odious little snob', and later as both a 'snob and a revolutionary'. People from his background — the Eton-educated 'aitch-pronouncing classes' — were brought up to think that working-class people were ignorant, lazy, drunken, boorish, dishonest, and smelly.[8] Orwell only managed to overcome these prejudices by confronting them and becoming aware of them. Typically, Orwell did it the hard way.

I want to digress for a moment and take you through part of Orwell's hard moral journey to reconnect with his fellow Englishmen and women. When he set off to Wigan and the north of England in the winter of 1936, Orwell was deadly serious about sharing real-life experiences with the poor. Few of them had warm overcoats, so he left his behind. And if they had to live in damp, unsanitary housing, so would he. His first two weeks were spent living in a slum lodging-house in Wigan — an experience that inspired some of his most memorable prose. Here is his brilliant description of life in the lodging-house:

> On the day when there was a full chamber-pot under the breakfast table I decided to leave. The place was beginning to depress me. It was not only the dirt, the smells, and the vile food, but the feeling of stagnant, meaningless decay, of having got down into some subterranean place where people got creeping round and round, just like blackbeetles, in an endless muddle of slovened jobs and mean grievances.[9]

It would be easy to blame slovenly and venal landlords for such living conditions, but Orwell wanted all of his fellow Englishmen to take some responsibility for the way people at the bottom of society were forced to live. He issued a challenge to journalists and writers to know what was happening in places such as Wigan:

> It's a kind of duty to see and smell such places now and again, especially smell them, lest you should forget that they exist; though perhaps it's best not to stay there too long.[10]

We have seen in chapter one how Orwell's belief that we share a common humanity has resonated with Australian intellectuals such as Robert Manne and Raymond Gaita. Orwell extended the principle not just to foreigners and enemy soldiers, but to people from within our own society and culture as well — the outcasts, the poor, and the affluent working class. One of Orwell's most celebrated passages in *The Road to Wigan Pier* is his description of the young working-class woman he saw from a train as he was leaving Wigan for the south:

> As we moved slowly through the outskirts of the town we passed row after row of little grey slum houses running at right angles to the embankment. At the back of one of the houses a young woman was kneeling on the stones, poking a stick up the leaden waste-pipe which ran from the sink inside and which I suppose was blocked. I had time to see everything about her — her sacking apron, her clumsy clogs, her arms reddened by the cold. She looked up as the train passed, and I was almost near enough to catch her eye. She had a round pale face, the usual exhausted face of the slum girl who is twenty-five and looks forty, thanks to miscarriages and drudgery; and it wore, for the second in which I saw it, the most desolate, hopeless expression I have ever seen. It struck me then that we are mistaken when we say that 'It isn't the same for them as it would be for us,' and that people bred in the slums can imagine nothing but the slums. For what I saw in her face was not the ignorant suffering of an animal. She knew well enough what was happening to her — understood as well as I did how dreadful a destiny it was to be kneeling there in the bitter cold, on the slimy stones of a slum backyard, poking a stick up a foul drain-pipe.[11]

Reading this passage as an impressionable eighteen-year-old was one of the things that turned me into the angry young man I've been trying hard to remain ever since. Orwell gets inside the minds of the people he meets, in ways that are still instructive. In the 1930s, as today, the well fed liked to sermonise to the poor and unemployed, stereotyping them as dole bludgers, and lecturing them on their poor diet — the sort of ratings fodder that today dominates programs such as *A Current Affair* and *60 Minutes*. Like them, the wealthy expect the poor to eat brown rice and vegetables by the handful but, of course, without the $30 bottle of wine to wash it down with. Here's Orwell responding to claims that the unemployed should spend their dole more wisely and eat more healthily:

> When you are unemployed, which is to say when you are underfed, harassed, bored, and miserable, you don't want to eat dull wholesome food. You want something a little bit 'tasty'. There is always some cheaply pleasant thing to tempt you. Let's have three pennorth of chips! Run out and buy us a twopenny ice-cream! Put the kettle on and we'll all have a nice cup of tea! That is how your mind works when you are at the P.A.C. (i.e. unemployment benefit) level.[12]

This is one of Orwell's many observations that give you the sense that he has really got below the skin of the working class and the poor to find out how we would think in their situation. Orwell was no day-tripper to an unemployment theme park. He met, lived with, and liked the people he wrote about. For some months he lived in coal miners' homes, ate meals with their families, washed at the kitchen sink (they often had no bathroom), shared bedrooms with miners, drank beer, played darts, and talked to them for hours on end. Perhaps the strange envy many have of people trapped on welfare would be less prevalent if some of our tabloid commentators made a similar effort to understand the lives of the less fortunate among us.

Earlier, I quoted Orwell's statement that while one should experience places like his Wigan boarding house, one shouldn't stay too long. He didn't take his own advice. At a time when many infectious diseases were rife among the poor and still incurable, living among them was highly dangerous. Orwell never shirked such dangers. Here's an excerpt from his diary detailing one of the houses he visited:

> House in Thomas Street. Back to back, two up, one down. Cellar below. Living-room 14 ft by 10 ft, and rooms above corresponding. Sink in living-room. Top floor has no door but gives on open stairs, walls in living-room slightly damp, walls in top rooms coming to pieces and oozing damp on all sides. House is so dark that light has to be kept burning all day. Electricity estimated at 6d. a day (probably an exaggeration). Six in family, parents and four children. Husband (on P.A.C.) is tuberculous. One child in hospital, the others appear healthy. Tenants have been seven years in this house. Would move, but no other house available. Rent 6s. 6d., rates included.[13]

Tuberculosis is recorded in other diary entries as well. All of

Orwell's books of reportage contain stories of sharing damp, confined places — doss houses, vile bed and breakfasts, dugouts in the front lines — with men with pallid faces and hacking coughs. It's probable that it was while pursuing the truth in one of these places that Orwell contracted the tuberculosis that killed him at the age of forty-six.

This was Orwell's version of getting 'inside the whale' — writing about what life is really like, not about what our ideologies tell us it should be. Having experienced their suffering and joy, Orwell empathised with the ordinary people of his day.

One can't imagine Orwell accepting a million dollars a year to rubbish unemployed families like the Paxtons, poke fun at fat kids on *A Current Affair*, or write front-page headlines for the Sydney *Daily Telegraph* describing razor-wire-encased desert refugee camps as luxury five-star resorts. Orwell had real journalistic integrity. He couldn't be tempted by riches. He lived on close to a labourer's income for much of his life. Midway through the Second World War he quit the BBC to become part-time literary editor of the socialist *Tribune*, even though it meant giving up the first middle-class income he'd earned since he'd been a policeman in Burma in the 1920s. By the time he could live off his royalties from the sales of *Animal Farm* and *Nineteen Eighty-Four* he was too sick from tuberculosis to enjoy them.

What mattered to Orwell wasn't money. (When asked by the American Book of the Month Club to make changes to *Nineteen Eighty-Four*, he refused on the grounds of artistic integrity, even though he was close to broke and it meant possibly losing the equivalent of twenty times an average middle-class salary, and more than 60 times what he earned the year he wrote *The Road to Wigan Pier.*)He once wrote that a writer should earn just enough to not have to be financially beholden to anyone, but not enough to lose sympathy for ordinary people. He even gave us a sum — £300 per year for an unmarried writer which, at roughly twice the annual wage of the lowest paid of his day, would translate to about $50,000 per year in our money.[14] It's roughly the starting salary of a university lecturer. He also said that the best income that would free a novelist from reviews and hackwork was £1,000, but he went on living the life of the hack reviewer until the day he died.

Do our journalists and writers today earn too much to have a real understanding of the lives of ordinary Australians? This is certainly true of the multi-million-dollar celebrity journalists on television and radio, but it's a more complex question than in Orwell's day. Today, many skilled tradespeople would earn as much if not more than a journalist. Perhaps I'm asking the wrong question because, regardless of their income level, few journalists today would inhabit the same world as the average member of the Australian working class. They live in separate suburbs, drink in separate pubs, drive on separate freeways. I want to give one — at first glance, frivolous — example to show what I mean. The following passage is from what was a regular popular-culture column by Melbourne *Age* journalist Corrie Perkin. In this column she tries to explain the ins and outs of Australian popular culture to her housemate, who is from California:

> You can pick a Kath and Kim fan a mile away. They launch into the lingo, just as Comedy Company fans did more than 10 years ago with Kylie Mole. They can tell you what each of the main characters wore during a certain scene. And they talk about going down to Fountain Gate for 'a chino and a bit of P and Q', as though the shopping mall is a real place.

As some indignant letter-writers to *The Age* pointed out, Fountain Gate shopping centre *is* a real place, and has been for about twenty years. It's on the left-hand side of the Princess Highway as you drive away from Melbourne, about ten kilometres from Dandenong, and it serves some of the fastest-growing suburbs in Australia, like Narre Warren and Berwick. This in itself is rather trivial; but when a cultural critic from Melbourne pokes fun at working-class culture from a point of such total ignorance, it highlights the lack of understanding between some of our journalists and their subjects. One correspondent put it well: 'Geographical mistakes like Perkin's ... give an impression that audiences outside the inner Melbourne core of Brighton, Balwyn and Brunswick are devalued by our metropolitan newspapers; that they are foreign and bizarre places, outside society.'[15] It seems Corrie Perkin has a better understanding of the Californian culture of her housemate than that of Melbourne's working-class south-eastern suburbs. But how can this be? How can a journalist who lives in Melbourne writing about Fountain Gate seemingly never have heard of it?

This ignorance of the outer suburbs has got something to do with a paradox that Orwell himself was aware of — that it's easier for a middle-class person to get to know beggars and foreigners than to get to know working-class people from their own country; indeed, from their own city or neighbourhood. As Orwell says, 'nothing is easier than to be bosom pals with a pickpocket, if you know where to look for him; but it is very difficult to be bosom pals with a bricklayer ... even a bishop could be at home among tramps if he wore the right clothes; and even if they knew he was a bishop it might not make any difference, provided that they also knew or believed that he was genuinely destitute.'

> But when you come to the normal working class the position is totally different. To begin with, there is no short cut into their midst. You can become a tramp simply by putting on the right clothes and going to the nearest casual ward, but you can't become a navvy or a coal-miner.[16]

Here's one of our most serious problems. It's easier to mix from within the extremes — of both class *and* culture — than to get to know an average, reasonably affluent working-class person. Where would you meet them, other than behind a counter, under the bonnet of your car, or at the wheel of a taxi? (At least Australians sit in the front passenger seat of cabs, which is something people don't do overseas.) By contrast, social workers or those who assist charities meet the destitute every day, talk with them at length, visit their homes, and know exactly what they're going through.

This ignorance of the lives and concerns of the majority of

working-class families damages our democracy. It's one of the reasons that the Hanson phenomenon took so many journalists and all mainstream political parties by surprise in 1996. It's also why too much of the criticism of mainstream political parties from the left and the right is so out of touch with reality. They are mainstream parties for a reason — they represent, albeit imperfectly and sometimes badly, the hopes and aspirations of the people in places like Fountain Gate. Let me give you one example of the kind of criticism that can be unfounded and unrealistic.

Since the 2001 election there have been numerous public debates about why John Howard won and what direction the mainstream left-wing parties — mainly Labor, but also the Democrats and Greens — should be taking. The debates have been joined enthusiastically by left-wing academics and journalists, often in a 'I told you so' manner. One thing that strikes me about such commentators is their poor grasp not just of the realities of politics (which I will come to shortly), but the realities of ordinary people's lives, especially the actual levels of working-class affluence and deprivation.

This was displayed well in a public debate in 2002 between the director of the Australia Institute, Clive Hamilton, and Ray Cassin, a left-wing journalist from the Melbourne *Age*. Hamilton argued that, contrary to accepted left-wing thinking, the dominant characteristic of contemporary Australia is not deprivation but abundance. He maintained that 'we thrive on the imagined wretchedness of others.' Here is how he described working-class affluence:

> By any standard Australia is an enormously wealthy country. The great majority of its citizens want for nothing. In 1950, average real incomes were around $9,000; today they are more than $30,000. Average households today are filled with big-screen TVs and DVDs. When we overfly the suburban expanses of Sydney, we see backyards dotted with swimming pools. It is nothing for an average parent to spend $1,000 on a present for a child or to buy them a personal mobile phone. Ordinary families happily shell out $40,000 for a four-wheel drive play-thing and gamble away a few thousand dollars each year merely for entertainment.

According to Hamilton, we are richer than ever before, but the pursuit of growth is making us unhappy. The central organising principle of the left should not be redistribution but encouraging people to opt out of the rat race.[17] Hamilton is, in short, asking the non-conservative parties to adopt the manifesto of the Greens. One of Hamilton's many critics was Ray Cassin. Cassin's key complaint was that, even if the really deprived comprised only 10 to 20 per cent of the population, that's still a good reason to try to make their life materially better. The strength of Cassin's argument is his personal knowledge of poorer communities in the northern suburbs of Melbourne, through his family's involvement in a Uniting Church community centre. It leads Cassin to dismiss Hamilton's claim that 'ordinary families' can afford $40,000 for a four-wheel drive:

> Hamilton did not bother too much about citing evidence for his assertions about general prosperity, such as, 'ordinary families

> happily shell out $40,000 for a four-wheel-drive plaything and gamble away a few thousand dollars each year merely for entertainment'. Ordinary, Clive? Spending $40,000 on a four-wheel-drive plaything doesn't seem very ordinary to me, but perhaps what is ordinary in the seminar rooms of Canberra think tanks is not what is ordinary in the working-class northern suburbs of Melbourne.[18]

As it happens, I think that they're both out of touch. To explain why, we need to revisit Corrie Perkin's nonsuch-place, Fountain Gate. Cassin is correct when he says that the affluence that buys $40,000 cars isn't the norm in Melbourne's northern suburbs — the statistics agree with him. According to the 2001 Census, the median weekly family income in the northern Melbourne suburb of Broadmeadows is only $30,572 per year. But such affluence *is* a reality in the working-class suburbs of Melbourne's south-east. In Narre Warren, for instance, where many of the shoppers at Fountain Gate live, median weekly family income is $51,948. The average for Australia is $48,724.

Don't be satisfied with the statistics, though; go there yourself and have a look. Do a test: take your car one Saturday or Sunday afternoon on a drive down the South-Eastern Freeway to Fountain Gate. Get in the middle lane and have a look at the cars in front, behind, and on either side. At least one will most likely be the equivalent of a luxury Toyota Landcruiser. If you're an academic or a journalist, don't be surprised if all of the cars are better than the dented one you're driving. It's a far cry from

Orwell's trip, without his winter coat, to the economically crushed north of England in 1936.

But, while we can't all be like George Orwell, we can get to know how our fellow citizens live, by trying just a little — which is the first step to making our democracy work for all of us. If you get to know some of the people of the Fountain Gate area you will find that, as Hamilton says, they often do have big-screen televisions and DVD players, commonly buy $40,000 four-wheel drives, frequently extend their homes, spend holidays in Bali, and even buy their children mobile phones for Christmas. Bottles of chardonnay and espresso machines can be found in their kitchens.

I know this, because Fountain Gate is where all of my immediate and most of my extended family do their shopping. That's how they live. They are not middle class and are not tertiary educated. They are working class; they all left school at fifteen, and work in factories and shops. They are members of unions, but far from politicised and militant. The affluence of the people who live around Fountain Gate may come and go according to the economic climate, and the cars may be bought on credit or with the proceeds of a redundancy cheque, but Hamilton's description is uncannily accurate.

Orwell went to Wigan to show the comfortable and educated upper-middle class of his day the almost universal destitution of the working classes during the Great Depression. Paradoxically, the lesson for us from his trip is the need to make the educated left aware of the surprising level of affluence that can be found is so many working-class communities in

Australia. The political importance of this task for the left lies in a simple equation. Poor and affluent working-class Australians — from unemployed indigenous Australians to low-paid migrant hotel cleaners, unskilled and semi-skilled factory workers, self-employed tradespeople, and white-collar call-centre workers — taken together add up to a majority of the electorate. Unless the left can command their allegiance, it has little future, and it has no chance of helping those at the very bottom.

That's where both Cassin and Hamilton, for separate reasons, lead us. Cassin's advice would have the centre-left pitching to too narrow an audience, leaving the relatively affluent working and lower-middle class to the bigoted dog-whistles of the right. And Hamilton's advice would prevent the centre-left from adequately tackling the evils of poverty, leaving the victims of economic change in the clutches of Hansonism, perhaps taking out their frustration and rage on those lower down the kicking order than them. This reliance on ideology rather than experience would seem to me to be one of the chief sources of the electoral weakness of the centre-left in Australia today. The centre-left needs a viable political strategy. It needs to be able to count to fifty-one. It needs to get real.

'If there is hope, it lies with the proles'

George Orwell was a man of the left. He hated poverty and he despised the lazy dividend-drawing class who ran England in their own interests. But, despite having passionately held socialist beliefs, he was no utopian. Christopher Hitchens has accurately emphasised the fact that one of Orwell's key traits was his left-wing contrarianism. In other words, it mattered not so much what he thought, but how he thought — independently, for himself, and without regard for the lures or enticements offered by power or money.[19] He was a man continually at an angle to society. Despite this, he was also a realist when it came to politics. In fact, much of Orwell's critique of intellectuals related to their naiveté as well as their power worship, and a lot of his politics related to the need of the centre-left to build a democratic majority so a reforming government could come to power through the ballot box, not violent revolution. We sometimes forget that this belief in democracy was the necessary flip side to Orwell's opposition to totalitarianism. Politically, he was willing to throw his support behind a radical but practical platform that would increase the living standards of the working class and dethrone the oligarchy that ran Britain.

If we're searching for a directly political lesson from Orwell, what would it be? It's obvious from the passage I quoted at the start of this chapter that Orwell would not have been a supporter of single-issue parties, and he would have been an unlikely supporter of the politics of 'rainbow coalitions'. In his own day, his allegiance was clear: he supported the Attlee Labour government, and he wanted the British Labour Party to be the party not just of left-wing intellectuals but the great mass of ordinary working people — from the very poorest to the working class and middle class. It would seem to me that this is Orwell's direct political legacy for the Australian centre-left, too.

Whether Labor, Democrat, or Green, Orwell's message would have been that they need to craft a reforming platform that could appeal to a numerical majority.[20]

Orwell never wasted his time searching for a mythical revolutionary working class, as many of his communist colleagues did, and as many left-wing critics of the Labor Party especially do today. In fact, Orwell did not think the working class were revolutionary at all — at least not in the sense of their being ready to rise up and seize the state. He considered the whole idea a fantasy, and sent the very notion of it up in a comic scene in *Nineteen Eighty-Four*. One day, while walking illicitly through the prole quarters of London, Winston Smith hears the shout of hundreds of voices, and immediately thinks that the great uprising has come at last. But when he looks closer he sees that it is merely a bunch of prole women fighting over cheap but scarce pots and pans at a market stall.[2]

Orwell understood that the real working class had more practical concerns than the fictional one found only in the ridiculous publications of left-wing intellectuals. Orwell sided firmly with the non-revolutionary working class. He was the first to admit that the patriotism and xenophobia of much of the working class was at odds with the tolerant, liberal internationalism of the socialist movement, but he persisted in his belief in the working class because he believed that, deep down, their *values* were ultimately at odds with those of their rulers.[22] This is the real meaning of Winston Smith's phrase that 'if there is hope, it lies with the proles'. 'Proles' today is, of course, a demeaning term, but there is still reason to believe that hope for political change in Australia still depends on tapping the egalitarian and redistributive sentiments and interests of ordinary, working Australians.

When Orwell wrote about the working class, it wasn't just about the poverty experienced by so many of its members. Being working class wasn't something that he wanted to destroy in order to make everyone middle class; he wanted more people to appreciate working-class culture and enjoy it. He admired working-class people for their toughness. He praised their way of life, and denounced unbridled capitalism because it denied the life of simple comfort to so many. Before his death, he wrote that he would be happy for his adopted son, Richard, to become a farmer, a sailor, a civil engineer, or something useful of that description, and that's exactly how it turned out.[23] Orwell was no snobby Bloomsbury socialist. Here's one of his most celebrated passages, from *The Road to Wigan Pier*:

> In a working-class home — I am not thinking at the moment of the unemployed, but of comparatively prosperous homes — you breathe a warm, decent, deeply human atmosphere which it is not so easy to find elsewhere. I should say that a manual worker, if he is in steady work and drawing good wages — an 'if' which gets bigger and bigger — has a better chance of being happy than an 'educated' man. His home life seems to fall more naturally into a sane and comely shape. I have often been struck by the peculiar easy completeness, the perfect symmetry as it were, of a working-class interior at its best. Especially on winter evenings after tea, when the fire glows in the open range and dances

> mirrored in the steel fender, when Father, in shirt-sleeves, sits in the rocking chair at one side of the fire reading the racing finals, and Mother sits on the other with her sewing, and the children are happy with a pennorth of mint humbugs, and the dog lolls roasting himself on the rag mat — it is a good place to be in, provided that you can be not only in it but sufficiently of it to be taken for granted ... Curiously enough it is not the triumphs of modem engineering, nor the radio, nor the cinematograph, nor the five thousand novels which are published yearly, nor the crowds at Ascot and the Eton and Harrow match, but the memory of working-class interiors — especially as I sometimes saw them in my childhood before the war, when England was still prosperous — that reminds me that our age has not been altogether a bad one to live in.[24]

This is in many ways an extraordinary passage. It does sound appealing, and it rings true, as anyone who has come from a happy and relatively prosperous working-class home will tell you. It is almost impossible to imagine one of the fashionable writers of the 1930s and 1940s, such as Evelyn Waugh, Anthony Powell, or numerous members of the Bloomsbury circle, writing with this easy familiarity about such things. And it's difficult also to think of a journalist or writer in Australia who can write with such intimacy about lives in comfortable, suburban working-class homes. (Note how feature articles in our newspapers and their glossy weekend magazines on subjects like the changing nature of work and the family always seem to have as their subjects interior designers, publicists, and writers — feature writers at least tend to move in limited circles.)

The first reaction of many on the left to such a passage is sometimes defensive. For too many intellectuals especially, working-class culture is understood only in stereotype: as a breeding ground of sexism, racism, and various forms of ignorance generally. There's a feeling that praising working-class family life is somehow an automatic criticism of non-traditional ways of living; that it's a roundabout way of being homophobic or against single mothers or of backing John Howard's prescriptive ideal of the two-parent family, safe from the contaminations of the outside world behind the barricade of the white picket fence. (Howard's ideal home was, in fact, a pitch not to the working class but his first run at an attempt to tap middle-class resentment and insecurity: the house would have contained a piano and sherry decanter, not the family dog and the racing form-guide.) There is no need to be prescriptive about the structure of the modern family, but I believe that our society would be better if more working-class families had a sufficient share of the nation's prosperity to enable them to live the modern-day equivalent of Orwell's happy home. Many aspire to the dream of Orwell's happy abode because it's a lot better than the social disaster afflicting many poorer working-class suburbs at present.

Again, emulate Orwell, and go and have a look. I recently returned to have a look at the street and house in the outer south-eastern suburb in which I grew up, and which I left more that twenty years ago. Our home was part of a new Housing Commission estate built in the mid-1960s to service the sprawling canning and vehicle-assembly plants along the Princess Highway. It was an estate clearly defined by its types of houses — a mixture of brick houses interspaced with concrete prefabs — that were cheap to build, but sturdy and functional. There were new local schools, a kindergarten, a fish-and-chip shop, an independent grocer, a chemist and a milk-bar, sporting ovals, and bus stops. It was highly multicultural *and* tolerant. It was an identifiable community. In much the same way that people in today's trendier suburbs such as St. Kilda or Glebe think of themselves as a neighbourhood or village, so did we.

Unfortunately, the reasonably happy and optimistic blue-collar community of my youth is no longer so prosperous. The street looks utterly forlorn, and my old home struck me as wretched looking — curtains still closed at 11.00 am, and rusted and broken-down cars in the now concreted-over front yard. There was little sign of any affluence at all. I felt a bit like Orwell who, when visiting the 1930s equivalents of such places, instinctively understood that something good had been lost, and that something mean and unnecessary had been put in its place. The city council and an influx of proud new home-buyers attracted to the cheap real estate are starting to improve things in my old area, but I doubt it will ever get back to its former glory without some bigger effort from national governments.

Why did Orwell think the values of the working class set them at odds with the rich and powerful? We can find part of his reasoning in his memorable essay on one of his favourite writers, Charles Dickens. Dickens' great achievement, Orwell thought, was 'to express in a comic, simplified and therefore memorable form the native decency of the common man' — the type of decency that can't be found in any ideology but 'in the impulse that makes a jury award excessive damages when a rich man's car runs over a poor man'.[25] (This is a common feature of our own times, and the real reason that insurance companies and their tabloid backers violently agitate for tort law reform to limit damages for personal injury.)

Orwell was drawn to Dickens' novel *Hard Times*. Although the novel is about the inhuman consequences of the industrial revolution in northern England, Dickens wasn't interested so much in changing economic systems as in changing human behaviour. The hero of the book — whose moral steadfastness set him at odds with the Gradgrinds of nineteenth-century capitalism — wasn't the revolutionary trade union leader. It was, rather, the humble factory hand Stephen Blackpool, who would have nothing to do with union organisers or left-wing politics, but who remained the decent and deeply human figure — someone who always stood up for the underdog. Orwell notes approvingly that Dickens was a revolutionary, but only in the moral sense. He was a moralist, not a politician. The very vagueness of his discontent was a mark of its permanence: he hated tyranny and unfairness, not this or that economic or political system.[26]

For this reason, Dickens, his character Stephen Blackpool and, of course, Orwell himself, were prepared to change sides when the underdog became the upperdog. (As Orwell did when the communists in Spain became the upperdogs of his day, thus providing the moral for *Animal Farm*.) In such passages,

Orwell's message to us is that the hope for change doesn't lie in trying to sell a new economic or political system, but rather in expressing the feeling for justice and fairness shared by ordinary people and reformers alike. It seems to me that, if Orwell's Dickens wrote about Australia today, his heroic characters wouldn't be left-wing lawyers or artists, but someone like a self-employed suburban baker who usually voted Labor (and perhaps, at the prompting of his teenage daughter, Green or Democrat in the Senate), and whose philosophy would be summed up by the term 'the fair go'.

This belief in the superior values of ordinary, everyday people was reflected in Orwell's own novels. In *A Clergyman's Daughter*, for instance, the central character, Dorothy, is saved from starvation by a family of hop-pickers who take pity on her fallen state.[27] In *Nineteen Eighty-Four* it's the prole women who are upset by the bombing of lifeboats full of refugee women and children. Contrast this with the very last diary entry that Orwell made just prior to his death, where he describes the overheard conversation of the unseen upper-class visitors of a neighbouring patient in his sanatorium:

> And what voices! A sort-of over-fedness, a fatuous self-confidence, a constant bah-bahing of laughter about nothing, above all a sort of heaviness and richness combined with a fundamental ill-will — people who, one instinctively feels, without even being able to see them, are the enemies of anything intelligent or sensitive or beautiful. No wonder everyone hates them so.[28]

This attitude of Orwell's is a good starting point for thinking about how we create a better Australia. The true spirit of Australia doesn't lie in the ranks of the chief executives who misuse their power to pay themselves outrageous salaries and golden handshakes. Ordinary Australians rightly despise such people, sensing that their gains are ill gotten — basically stolen from the people who do all the hard work — and that they must be truly stupid if they think their money can buy them a gold-carpeted stairway to heaven. But it's this selfish minority who currently have access to our national leaders.

The real Australia lies in the suburbs, where people, although intermittently under financial pressure, nonetheless manage to feed, clothe, educate, and love their kids; pay their mortgages and monthly bills; get on cheerfully with their neighbours, no matter where they're from or what their culture; and enjoy barbeques, the footy, shopping for new things at places like Fountain Gate, and reading the *Women's Weekly*. And while the Tampa episode may have revealed a darker side, one of the causes for optimism is surely the way that people generally accept their own neighbours as good people, no matter how different their culture may be. It always seems to be the case that 'the Muslim/Vietnamese/Pacific Islander neighbours in *our* street are good people'. The good side of Australians is there for political leaders to appeal to.

To Clive Hamilton, such suburban lives may seem slightly vulgar and materialistic. But there are worse ways to live, and many people who live in the suburbs are well able to appreciate art and literature, write poetry, and develop a thoughtful philosophy of how to live the good life. (Ronald Reagan's former speechwriter, Peggy Noonan, wrote in her memoirs that people in politics too often forget the simple fact that anyone who has reached the later years of high school has at least one favourite piece of serious literature that helps them interpret the world around them. Recently at a party I talked to a tradesman who is an expert on Ernest Hemingway, and thinks nothing of driving for hours to second-hand bookshops in the country to collect a first edition.)

It seems to me that many of our social problems and prejudices arise not when there is an abundance of comfortable working-class affluence, but when it is missing because of chronic unemployment, accidents, ill-health, or low aspirations — as today in my old home town. It's the values and aspirations of these ordinary and affluent Australians to which the Australian centre-left must appeal. While it may be true that Australians are collectively less socially minded today than twenty years ago, the inclination to care for our fellow citizens is still an essential element of suburban Australian culture. Go to the suburbs, talk to with the people, and find out for yourself. As the economist Lindy Edwards puts it in her recent book, *How to Argue with an Economist*, the cultural values that led Australian soldiers imprisoned in Changi to bond together, and share their last bag of rice when the going got rough, is in our bones and will be ground down with us when we die.[29]

When Kim Beazley said in his poignant and tragic concession speech on election night 2001 that the political challenge for the centre-left was to appeal to 'the good angels of our nature', these are the things he was talking about. The recent political and intellectual fashion of transforming 'the fair go' from 'caring for others' into its opposite — 'caring for ourselves only' — demonstrates Orwell's warning that when words lose their meaning unscrupulous politicians can convince us that two plus two equals five.

In the short term, Australia's conservatives may have triumphed electorally by appealing to our bleaker angels. But this set of decent suburban values, this native sense of common decency, will reassert itself eventually. All that's needed is a political program that can draw it out and mobilise it for the common good. And the first step to achieving this is building understanding and sympathy between the centre-left's educated leadership and the people themselves. We have to learn to speak the same language again. This is precisely where it gets difficult.

My Australia, right or left

Does Orwell offer us any sort of program for the future? He wrote a political manifesto of sorts only once — in his essay 'The Lion and the Unicorn'. Penned during the Battle of Britain and the Blitz in 1940 and 1941 (and opening with that memorable line — 'As I write enemy planes are flying overhead trying to kill me'), 'The Lion and the Unicorn' argued that England's best hope of winning the war — in which she then stood alone against formidable odds — was to unleash the energy of the entire population through a social and political revolution that swept away the authority of the old and generally incompetent ruling class. It argued for the nationalisation of land, mines, railways, banks, and major industries; a limitation of incomes so that no one was allowed to earn more than ten times the minimum wage; democratic reform of the education system; Indian independence; and reforms to the way the war was being conducted to include the 'coloured' countries of the British Empire. What seemed revolutionary in 1940 was called reform by 1945, when the Attlee Labour government implemented a program strikingly similar to Orwell's.

There is still some lasting relevance today, especially the calls for more equality of income and educational opportunities, and greater assistance for developing nations, but it's the intent behind Orwell's program that has continuing relevance. Orwell believed that an England ruled in the interests of a narrow clique drawn from the top public (that is, 'private') schools could not hope to win the war. Echoing John Milton's pamphlets defending the English republic of the 1640s, Orwell wanted to use the urgency of the war to force through reforms that would unleash the native genius of the English people in the fight against fascism. This did not mean red flags and proletarian dictatorship, but a uniting of the working and middle classes against the choking of talent and industry of the whole population under the narrow rentier class that still ran England in the 1940s. 'Right through our national life', Orwell argued, 'we have got to fight against the notion that a half-witted public schoolboy is better for command than an intelligent mechanic.'[30]

What could be more relevant to Australia today? In an era

when our nation has to live by its wits, when our long-term security and prosperity depends on the education and skills of our people, Australia can only hope to reach its full potential when everyone's abilities are unleashed. Every day we see more evidence of what Orwell saw in the ruling class of his day: venality, untruthfulness, incompetence, and backward vision. Whether it's the findings of the HIH royal commission or massive handouts to wealthy private schools and private health insurance firms, it's obvious that the rewards are going to fewer Australians, and that the nation's talent is being recruited from a much smaller social circle. An inbred and inter-married national leadership drawn from the Category 1 private schools, attended by the wealthiest 2 per cent of the population, is a backward step for the nation. But that's where we're headed.

Unleashing the talent of the Australian people can't be done just by saying we want to do it; it takes hard political work. It can only happen when the centre and the left get back into national government, and that will only happen when there is once again a solid alliance between blue-collar Australians and the progressive-minded, tertiary-educated middle class. Over the last decade, culminating at the 2001 federal election, these two social groupings, which historically have supported Labor, have been driven apart by a combination of ruthless wedge politics on the right and disillusionment with practical parliamentary politics on the left. These two groups must come together in a progressive coalition if the country is to move forward again.

Orwell believed that the intellectual left had a moral obligation to try to connect with ordinary people and with the political system. The left, he thought, was wasting too much energy in debates about fine matters of principle, and it had too high a regard for its own bourgeois sensibilities. When people in places like Wigan were living in destitution, and fascism was on the march, the left needed to channel its energies into gaining power. In his day, that meant getting behind a Labour party with reforming policies. In short, the left had to do two things: it had to connect with the culture and aspirations of the great mass of the people; and it had to embrace practical politics. Orwell's two challenges to the left are just as relevant today in Australia as they were in England in his own time.

The stumbling block is that anyone who moves regularly in both camps will tell you that the cultural distance between tertiary-educated left-wing intellectuals and suburban Australians has never been wider. By and large, they read different newspapers, listen to different radio stations, holiday in separate places and, most important of all, despite having a general hostility to the status quo, are obsessed by different political issues. It's perhaps best summed up as 'mutual incomprehension'.

The Australian left has many heroes — articulate spokespeople who write for the quality broadsheets, and are guests on Radio National, and do pro-bono work for worthy causes. But it's obvious that they're not connecting. The Australian left needs new heroes whose ideas are grounded in a real knowledge of the everyday realities of the lives of the majority of people. Too many of the figures held up in Australia as 'left' occupy a very narrow, if politically divided, slice of Australian society. They are usually just a touch too elitist and eccentric: more Vanessa Woolf than

George Orwell; more Bloomsbury than Fountain Gate. It's this gap in cultural understanding that John Howard has succeeded in driving a wedge through to break apart the centre-left's blue-collar and white-collar constituencies.

This isn't a call for a Maoist exodus of tertiary-educated and politically aware people to the outer suburbs, or for them to give up their appreciation of art and books and other aspects of highbrow culture. The answer is for all of us to acknowledge our level of disconnection from the lives of the vast majority, and make an effort to understand. Like so many, I live in an inner-city suburb; unlike most, I also spend part of my time writing speeches in the Parliament building in the sometimes-unreal power centre of Canberra. So, in more ways than one, I'm writing from a glasshouse. It *is* possible, however, to force oneself to keep in touch with the world outside. For me, this task is relatively easy; all I need to do is visit my family near Fountain Gate.

But even those from the most privileged backgrounds should be able to do it easily. George Orwell went to Eton, but even he managed to connect. There's no science to it. It means making an attempt to listen and keeping an open mind to the opinions of your fellow citizens, especially those outside the invisible social boundaries that surround you. And, if you disagree with them, try to understand why they think the way they do. Often, even including incredibly divisive and morally fraught issues such as refugees and welfare fraud, opposing opinions are motivated not by malice but an underlying outraged sense of justice to which people on the left should be attuned.

Much of this problem — the widening cultural and political

gap between blue-collar and white-collar Australians — is the centre-left's own fault. It has been far too willing to concede certain popularly held and worthwhile sentiments to the right. Take patriotism, for example. Phoney right-wing populists such as Pauline Hanson, who literally wrap themselves in the flag, have given patriotism a bad name. Left-wingers often wrongly regard patriotism as a front for conservatism. Patriotism is a hard sell for the left, but it doesn't have to be. Orwell grasped this point in *The Lion and the Unicorn*:

> Patriotism has nothing to do with Conservatism. It is actually the opposite of Conservatism, since it is a devotion to something that is always changing and yet is felt to be mystically the same. It is the bridge between the future and the past. No real revolutionary has ever been an internationalist.[31]

Orwell is right. Right-wing commentators have tried to use Orwell's well-known distinction between aggressive 'nationalism' and defensive 'patriotism' against the Australian left. The right are wrong in asserting that patriotism is what John Howard and the Liberals are trying to appeal to — it's nationalism. The right, in fact, do not care much for defending the truly 'Australian' egalitarian achievement. Waving the flag is for them an exercise in itself; merely a distraction to get us looking elsewhere while they take from us the hard-won gains of previous generations. It's the Australian left that must project itself as the true bastion of Australian patriotism. One must never succumb to the propagandists opposing our so-called 'black armband' historians, who want to deny the negative aspects of our past; but there is much in Australia's national past for people on the left to be proud of.

A colleague once made an interesting point to me that there is something about Australian life that would definitely appeal to George Orwell — our lack of an overt class system, our hatred of pretension, our practical reforming bent, and our belief, until recently at any rate, of the nation-building potential of government. All this adds up to a sort of socialism without ideology. The writer Edmund Campion has recently made the same point.[32] This national sentiment of egalitarianism, summed up in the slogan of 'the fair go', is a patriotic ideal that could unite all Australians from all backgrounds. It's our native genius that needs to be unleashed if Australia is to flourish. Orwell had a particularly wonderful analogy through which the left should understand patriotism. England, he wrote, was a family with the wrong members in control.[33] It would seem to me that the centre-left could do worse than think of Australia in the same way — proud of the country, but wanting its better-natured members determining its fate.

Getting real

The second main challenge for the Australian centre-left is to become more politically realistic and hard headed — to get real. Unlike the tabloid commentators on the right and the intellectuals of the left, most people are not motivated by ideology (or malice). Their political views are overwhelmingly practical. This is something you will inevitably find once you make the moral effort to connect. That's why so much democratic politics gravitates towards the centre — people want outcomes, not utopias.

Australian left intellectuals once spoke this same practical language. From the 1940s to the 1980s many of them (some under the influence of Orwell, as we have seen in chapter one) were involved in nation-building programs — from post-war reconstruction under Chifley and Menzies to the Whitlam and Hawke reforms. They planned the post-war immigration program, the creation of new industries, universal health cover, and the expansion of tertiary education. But something has gone seriously wrong. Too many centre-left intellectuals have lost their interest in practical politics and have stopped speaking the language of ordinary people, leaving the project of nation-building in the hands of free-market economists and soulless bureaucrats. As the American writer Todd Gitlin has said of the U.S. left: while academics were marching on the English Department, the Republicans were marching on the White House.[34]

By cutting themselves off — physically as well as psychologically — from life in the suburbs, Australia's centre-left intellectuals have missed the big increase in affluence and new patterns of poverty that have transformed the working class over the last twenty years. You can see it in the work of Ray Cassin and Clive Hamilton, as well as by reading any academic journal. If they emulated Orwell and made a serious effort to keep in touch with the people, they would find that the working class's political agenda has changed. We're at the birth of a new era of social-democratic politics. Just as Whitlam increased opportunities for working-class people to go to university and gain social mobility, the new social-democratic agenda is not only to rebuild damaged public institutions but to redistribute wealth and human capacities (not just income) through new means. This is not the subject of this short book, but new ideas abound that can fill this gap. You can find them in books like those by Mark Latham, Lindsay Tanner, and others, where the attempt is made to create 'big picture' reforms that are relevant to our changing lives and politically realistic at the same time.

Democracy is a difficult game, but one we must play. Unfortunately, too many on the left have a disdain for the realities of parliamentary and electoral politics — something recognised long ago by Orwell's biographer Bernard Crick, in his book *In Defence of Politics*. We should have no illusions about it — parliamentary politics is a sometimes-messy business. It involves heartbreaking compromises, and we often have to settle for half a loaf instead of none. But we can't and shouldn't try to escape it. Insisting on all or nothing, with no reference to public opinion is, in a sense, giving up. Orwell was right when he remarked that 'every revolutionary opinion draws part of its strength from a secret conviction that nothing can be changed.'[35] It's the politics of defiant empty gestures and egotistical showboating.

There are encouraging signs. The new radical social movements are finding articulate champions and gaining a voice in our parliamentary system. Where the election of centre-left candidates isn't viable, tough and independent-minded community-based candidates are being elected. But there is still a problem that must be honestly confronted: gaining a parliamentary majority for the anti-coalition parties as the first necessary step to saving of Australia's egalitarian way of life. While it seems likely and desirable that independents and the Greens will remain in the parliament, creating a fairer society will require the election of a Labor government. It's the reality that, Orwell was fond of saying, is right in front of our noses if we want to see it. Everyone opposed to the direction in which the coalition and its neo-conservative backers are taking the country has to consider a viable political and electoral strategy for tipping them out. This means, to an extent, reassessing their attitude to Labor.

Some of Labor's fiercest critics today come from the left. This is understandable; the culture wars and ugly wedge politics pushed by Australia's neo-conservatives throw up painful dilemmas with the power to divide. That's the whole point of using them. But it can be a trap that the centre-left sometimes leaps into with eyes wide open. Right-wing commentators always back the conservative parties to the hilt, showing unbending loyalty. But commentators on the centre-left seldom back Labor. In fact, attacks on the Labor Party from the left often make those by the right-wing tabloid commentators I wrote of in the last chapter seem tame. Here's a prime example from the novelist and prominent Tasmanian green activist Richard Flanagan, published on the eve of the 2001 federal election, which demonstrates the fraught moral and political challenges created for the centre-left by wedge politics. Flanagan is referring to Labor's border-protection policies and Kim

Beazley's refusal to call for the reuniting of the mother and father of three young girls who were drowned on the SIEV X:

> The ALP had long ago established that its venality and chicanery were beyond doubt, but this callousness without care for the consequences was new and horrifying. Labor tried to pretend it was about domestic issues. But the only job they were after was a job for the big puffy boy who, with his one great ironical gift, that of diminishment, managed to make a national election sound like a botched pitch for the job of assistant manager of a bottleshop — oh yes, he was qualified all right, he and his mates, conceited bastards all born to rule as much as those they derided on the government benches; the only health they cared for that of their pirates' fortune depicted in the polling charts; the only education they knew the re-education of any who dissented with a line that now so resembled the Liberals that only girth and eyebrows could be used to distinguish foe from friends.[36]

Ad hominem attacks don't get much more vicious than this. The Liberals — with their references to Labor leader Kim Beazley as a 'flip flopper' — at least had the good grace to be subliminal in their references to his weight. (Flanagan has a history of this, on another occasion referring to Beazley as 'a lost Zeppelin in search of a breeze'.[37]) The pretentious prose aside, this passage sums up the often counter-productive commentary of the intellectual left today — they believe that there's no significant difference on any issue between the major parties, and they have a tendency to attack Labor, not the coalition, whenever the latter resorts to dirty wedge politics.

Flanagan isn't alone. A day seldom passes without an article on the op ed pages from a centre-left commentator attacking Labor for its weakness and lack of beliefs. While well intentioned, contributions like these seem to me to be more than just a little artless. They conjure up the vision of an angry old man waving his fists and yelling his rage at the television news. It's bad for the soul, embittering, and a waste of energy. In fact, it's exactly the reaction from the left that the neo-conservatives were hoping for when Howard sent the SAS on to the Tampa. The neo-conservative intention is always the same: to split Labor's blue-collar voters from its tertiary-educated supporters, and to portray Labor as weak and standing for nothing. (It's a strategy that political professionals recognise as Nixon's 'southern strategy' from the 1960s and 1970s.) Too often, centre-left commentators help reinforce and illustrate that message.

Labor was certainly faced with a tough moral choice over the Tampa wedge, but to reward the Howard government for playing the race card by punishing Labor at the ballot box solved nothing. The reaction of people such as Flanagan is an example of an observation that Orwell once made, that the publications of the intellectual left are generally negative and querulous, and display a complete lack at all times of any constructive suggestion. 'There is little in them except the irresponsible carping of people who have never been and never expect to be in a position of power.'[38]

Differences of opinion within the anti-conservative forces are healthy and inevitable. This refusal to blindly support any political party is an undoubted intellectual strength, and a sign of the integrity on the centre-left that many on the right lack. But how do we get real about the practical task of getting back into power? Many think it needs a cringing *mea culpa* from Labor and a violent swing to the left. This is not the answer; it would simply play into the conservatives' hands again. The fault lies with the left for being politically naïve and culturally out of touch, just as much as the left thinks it lies with Labor for losing part of its religion. You can be realistic and compassionate at the same time.

The example exists in Orwell's life: always try to connect with and speak to ordinary people without surrendering your passion for equality; reject false utopias; and embrace the world of democratic politics, with all the tough choices that that entails. This can be done. The values of the centre-left are the mainstream values of Australians — the values we refer to collectively as 'the fair go'. If the conservatives can paint themselves as the champions of ordinary Australians, when their agenda is the opposite of egalitarianism, imagine what a united centre-left can achieve when it makes an effort to connect. The centre-left has the people to win this important battle for the hearts and minds of Australians — people who are more independent-minded, more compassionate and more like the real George Orwell than the neoconservative propagandists who now dominate public debate. It's time to get the battle on and fight, using our heads as well as our hearts, our reason as well as our passion.

CHAPTER FOUR

Postscript: the political adviser and leviathan today

I want to end on a personal note. There's a certain presumptiveness in writing an essay on George Orwell, one of the greatest political essayists of all time; and, many would argue, there's no small degree of irony in doing so while employed as a political adviser.

Orwell's view of political intellectuals wasn't high. They were usually the villains of his books and essays — ugly and unemotional, with a sharp little features and pince-nez spectacles, one day writing propaganda, the next operating the dials of a torture machine. But Orwell was not against writers becoming involved in politics, even party politics. He makes this clear in his 1948 essay *Writers and Leviathan*, in which he partly tries to make sense of his strong support for the Attlee Labour government, despite its mid-term disappointments. It's a complicated argument, but it comes down to this: writers can be involved in politics, campaign for a party, and even write about politics in a crude and technical way, but they should never do so *as a writer.*[1] A writer has one master — the truth, which should never be compromised. Party-political partisanship must be left at the office, and forgotten when the notebook and pen come out on the tram and the home computer is switched on during holidays and weekends.

That's what I've tried to do here. That's not to say that a political adviser who aspires to intellectual status is allowed to lie during office hours. If this is a politically engaged book, that's because I believe strongly — after work as well as during it — that there's nothing dishonest or anti-democratic about involvement in practical politics. Political advisers are a (sometimes unfortunate) necessity in modern politics. This was as true in Orwell's day as in ours, although there are a lot more of us today (and the comparison with Orwell's day is, anyway, a stretch: the apparatchiks Orwell attacked were, after all, communists in an era when the threat of totalitarianism was very real). Our political system would be better off if more advisers had a commitment to the values that Orwell espoused and, more importantly, lived. One can support a political party professionally or even as a common citizen, but never lie for it; or at least never do so and expect to be taken seriously as an intellectual. One should strongly argue a case, yes, but never knowingly lie or cover up the truth. If I were ever called upon professionally to lie, I would resign. The same can't be said of everyone in my profession, as I will touch on below.

My discovery of Orwell coincided with my interest in politics. Like most, I first read him at school — *Nineteen Eighty-Four* and *Animal Farm*. When I went to university and joined the Labor Party, his influence came back, courtesy of a long and dull holiday, stranded without a car in an outer-suburban housing estate. To escape boredom I read Orwell — novels and essays — until I'd read every page available in paperback. They're the same dog-eared Penguins I've used for this essay. I've never regretted reading a page, even though my friends were where I probably should have been — on the beach. I quickly developed a guilty conscience about some of my own behaviour as a student politician. Orwell's influence at least prevented me from committing worse youthful excesses. After completing my undergraduate degree, I was the guest of friends in the village of Shiplake, near Henley-on-Thames in England, and was surprised to find that their house was opposite the one in which the young Eric Arthur Blair grew up. A fascinating personal tour of the house and the places nearby sealed a lifelong interest. Ever since, whether writing about East Timor or economic rationalism, or through my involvement in promoting democratic reform of the ALP, Orwell's ideals have never been far from the surface.

Orwell's writings taught me lessons I'm more determined to obey the older I get: don't live in an ivory tower; don't let factions tell you what to think or do or how to vote; be suspicious of ideologies; reject orthodoxies of all kinds; stand at an angle to our society as long as it remains unfair; fearlessly pursue the truth; and never knowingly tell a lie. They're lessons that all political advisers — and all citizens — should try to obey, especially now, as advisers are becoming more powerful. The best advisers do obey these lessons. They're the ones with the most to offer, with the best ideas and with the courage to challenge us all — citizens, public servants, and elected politicians — to lift our game. Unfortunately, though, not all try to live by these rules. Some of the chief offenders in the greatest scandal to hit our political system in decades, the 'children overboard' affair, were political advisers. Their behaviour mocked our democracy and demonstrated the importance of the truth to the integrity of our democratic system. They helped clinch a stolen election and, now it seems, justify a war by recourse to a lie. Far from being held to account or falling on their swords, they've been promoted and rewarded, and still plague our politics. Unless they are ultimately brought to account, the precedent of their success will send our democracy into a downward spiral in which anything goes, racial division is freely exploited, ruthlessness triumphs and, inevitably, more corpses pile up. One day, they will be called to account when the truth is finally exposed. But, in the meantime, in the public interest, perhaps they should take a long, dull holiday and read George Orwell. We'd all be better off if they did.

Acknowledgements

I would like to thank a number of people whose discusssions with me and comments on earlier drafts contributed importantly to this book: Chris Barrett, Andrew Leigh, Mac Duncan, Michael Cooney, Melissa Lane, Michael Gurr, James Glover, and Fiona Hehir. All errors are, of course, mine alone.

Notes

Chapter One

1 Unless otherwise footnoted, this chapter is based on interviews with the major subjects by the author and Professor John McLaren in 1996–7. Tapes of these interviews (with the exception of that with Peter Ryan, who declined to have his interview taped) are stored in the library of the Footscray campus of Victoria University. Notes of interviews can be made available by contacting the author. The author acknowledges the support of the Australian Research Council for some of this research.

2 Timothy Garton Ash, 'Orwell in 1998', *New York Review of Books*, 22 October 1998, p. 11.

3 K. S. Inglis, *Observing Australia 1959 to 1999* (ed. Craig Wilcox), Melbourne University Press, Melbourne, 1999, p. 23.

4 K. S. Inglis, *The Stuart Case*, Melbourne University Press, Parkville, 1961; *Observing Australia*, p. 62.

5 Inglis, 'Multiculturalism and National Identity', in *Observing Australia*, pp. 186–219.

6 John Button, *As it Happened*, Text, Melbourne, 1998, pp. 62–4.

7 John Button, *As it Happened*, 125.

8 K. S. Inglis (ed.), *Nation: The Life of an Independent Journal of Opinion 1958–1972*, Melbourne University Press, Melbourne, 1989, pp. 2, 6, 251.

9 Peter Coleman, *Memoirs of a Slow Learner*, Angus and Robertson, Sydney, 1994, p. 38.

10 Coleman, *Memoirs of a Slow Learner*, pp. 46–7.

11 Norman Podhoretz, 'If Orwell Were Alive Today', *Quadrant*, October 1983; Peter Coleman, 'Confucian Hilarity', *Quadrant*, May 1999, p. 76.

12 Lauchlan Chipman, 'The Zealots: Australia's Thought Police', *Quadrant*, May 1984.

13 The following is drawn from Frank Knopfelmacher, 'My Political Education', *Quadrant*, July–August 1995 (originally published in *Quadrant*, July–August 1967) and Frank Knopfelmacher, 'Nineteen Eighty–Four', *Quadrant*, January–February 1984.

14 Peter Coleman (Obituary for Heinz Arndt), 'From Left to All Right', *The Australian*, 14 May 2002.

15 George Orwell, *The Collected Essays, Journalism and Letters of George Orwell* (hereafter *CEJL*), Vol. 4, (ed. Sonia Orwell and Ian Angus), Penguin, Harmondsworth, 1970, p. 276.
16 Simon Leys, *The Death of Napoleon*, Allen and Unwin, 1992 (first pub. in French as *La Mort de Napoleon*, 1986), p. 20.
17 Simon Leys, *The Angel and the Octopus: Collected Essays 1983–1998*, Duffy and Snellgrove, Sydney 1999, p. 55.
18 *The Angel and the Octopus*, pp. 143–4.
19 Simon Leys, *The Chairman's New Clothes: Mao and the Cultural Revolution*, St Martin's Press, New York, 1977 (first pub. 1971), p. 7.
20 Simon Leys, *Chinese Shadows*, The Viking Press, New York, 1977, p. 52, n. 8.
21 *Chinese Shadows*, esp. pp. 140–1 and 166.
22 Leys, *The Chairman's New Clothes*, p. 21.
23 Leys, *Chinese Shadows*, pp. 25–6.
24 Pierre Ryckmans, *The View from the Bridge, Aspects of Culture, The 1996 Boyer Lectures*, ABC Books, Sydney, 1996, p. 19.
25 Leys, *The Chairman's New Clothes*, pp. 13–54. Robert Manne, *The Shadow of 1917*, Text, Melbourne, pp. 169–181.
26 Leys, *Chinese Shadows*, p. xvi.
27 Interview with Luke Slattery, *The Weekend Australian*, 13–14 March 1999, p. 10.
28 Robert Manne, 'My Country: A Personal Journey', *The Alfred Deakin Lectures*, ABC Books, 2001, p. 544.
29 Robert Manne, *The Shadow of 1917: Cold War Conflict in Australia*, Text, Melbourne, 1994, pp. 16–19.
30 Manne, *The Shadow of 1917*, pp. 240–1.
31 Robert Manne, *The Culture of Forgetting: Helen Demidenko and the Holocaust*, Text, 1996.
32 Manne, *The Shadow of 1917*, p. 17.
33 Robert Manne, *The Way We Live Now. Controversies of the Nineties*, Text, Melbourne, 1998, p. 3.
34 Manne, *The Way We Live Now*, p. 278.
35 Robert Manne, 'George Orwell: To Say I Accept', *Melbourne University Magazine*, 1969, p. 32.
36 Manne, *The Shadow of 1917*, pp. 241 and 245.
37 Robert Manne, 'In Denial: The Stolen Generations and the Right', *Quarterly Essay*, no. 1, 2001, p. 57.
38 Raimond Gaita, *A Common Humanity: Thinking About Love and Truth and Justice*, Text, Melbourne, 1999, pp. 48–9, 57–72 and 120–1.
39 Gaita, *A Common Humanity*, pp. 188–9.
40 Gaita, *A Common Humanity*, p. 195.

Chapter Two

1 'Politics and the English Language', in *Inside the Whale and other essays*, p. 157.

2 George Orwell, *Homage to Catalonia*, Penguin, Harmondsworth, 1980, p. 144; 'Looking Back on the Spanish War', in *Homage to Catalonia*, p. 234 and p. 235.

3 Jeffrey Meyers, *Orwell: Wintry Conscience of a Nation*, W.W. Norton & Company, New York, 2000, pp. 38 and 172.

4 George Orwell, *The Road to Wigan Pier*, Penguin, Harmondsworth, 1962, p. 161; 'Inside the Whale', in George Orwell, *Inside the Whale and other essays*, Penguin, Harmondsworth, 1978, p. 31 and pp. 36–7.

5 Christopher Hitchens, *Orwell's Victory*, Allen Lane, London, 2002, pp. 146–50.

6 David Marr and Marian Wilkinson, *Dark Victory*, Allen and Unwin, Crows Nest, 2003, pp. 243, 244, 247–9, 266–9, 271, 276.

7 See transcripts at the home pages of the Prime Minister, Treasurer and Defence Minister: http://www.pm.gov.au/news/interviews/2002/interview1597.htm;
http://www.pm.gov.au/news/interviews/2002/interview1599.htm;
http://www.treasurer.gov.au/tsr/content/transcripts/2002/018.asp; and
http://www.minister.defence.gov.au/Hilltpl.cfm?CurrentId=1389.

8 George Orwell, *Nineteen Eighty–Four*, Penguin, Harmondsworth, 1979, pp. 10–11.

9 The Senate, *Select Committee on A Certain Maritime Incident, Report*, Commonwealth of Australia, October 2002, p. 73.

10 The Senate, *Select Committee on A Certain Maritime Incident, Report*, p. 478.

11 Letter to the Editor, *The Age*, 8 July 2003.

12 Bob Ellis, 'The Age of Spin', *Overland* 169, Summer 2002; Robert Manne, 'Unthinkable Brutality? Who cares?', *The Age*, 29 April 2002; *The Canberra Times*, 8 May 2003.

13 *Courier Mail*, 5 October 2003.

14 Marr and Wilkinson, *Dark Victory*, p. 51.

15 Ramonal Koval, *The Weekend Australian*, 27 May 2000.

16 George Orwell, *Coming Up for Air*, Penguin, Harmondsworth, 1962, p. 27.

17 George Orwell, 'England Your England', in *Inside the Whale and other essays*, p. 64.

18 Orwell, *Nineteen Eighty–Four*, pp. 46–7; see how Orwell had thought of this earlier in 'Politics and the English Language', in *Inside the Whale and other essays*, p. 152.

19 P. P. McGuinness, 'Wilting flower children get serious about aging', *Sydney Morning Herald*, 22 March 2001; Andrew Bolt, 'Mourn, don't blame', *Herald Sun*, 17 October 2002; Piers Akerman, 'Sinking ships and dirty Labor tricks', *The Daily Telegraph*, 24 October 2002;
Piers Akerman, 'Australians will not stand idly by', *The Daily Telegraph*, 5 December 2002.
20 Louis Menand, 'Honest, Decent, Wrong: The Invention of George Orwell', *The New Yorker*, 21 January 2003, p. 91.
21 Orwell, 'Politics and the English Language', in *Inside the Whale and other essays*, p. 156.
22 George Orwell, 'Notes on Nationalism', in *Decline of the English Murder and other essays*, Penguin, Harmondsworth, 1975, pp. 165, 166, 178.
23 Orwell, 'Inside the Whale', in *Inside the Whale and other essays*, p. 37.
24 George Orwell, 'Benefit of Clergy', in *Decline of the English Murder and other essays*, pp. 26–7.
25 P. P. McGuinness, 'Truth, sentiment and genocide as a fashion statement', *Sydney Morning Herald*, 14 September 2000.
26 *Sunday Herald Sun*, 19 May 2002; Piers Akerman, 'How we have been branded kidnappers', *The Sunday Mail*, 19 May 2002.
27 Andrew Bolt, 'You hypocrite, Phil', *Herald Sun*, 12 December 2002.
28 Gerard Henderson, 'Even quiet Americans face extreme prejudice', *The Age*, 4 February 2003.
29 Evan Williams, 'Journey into a nation's soul', *The Australian*, 23 February 2003.
30 Clive James, 'The All of Orwell', *The New Yorker*, 18 January 1999.
31 Andrew Bolt, 'Looney uni cuts', *Herald Sun*, 28 April 2003; Andrew Bolt, 'Footscray's Kremlin', *Herald Sun*, 21 April 2003; Andrew Bolt, 'Uncivilised art just crude political propaganda', *Herald Sun*, 23 June 2003; Andrew Bolt, 'You pay, she complains', *Herald Sun*, 12 June 2003; Andrew Bolt, 'A kick up the arts', *Herald Sun*, 2 June 2003; Andrew Bolt, 'Hitler: Green Guru', *Herald Sun*, 17 July 2003.
32 George Orwell, 'The Prevention of Literature', in *Inside the Whale and other essays*, pp. 169, 168.
33 John Howard, 'Some Thoughts on the Liberal party Philosophy in the 1990s', *Quadrant*, July–August 1994, p. 21.
34 See, for instance: Gerard Henderson, 'Howard is losing the Cultural War', *Sydney Morning Herald*, 8 October 2002; Gerard Henderson, 'The Liberals have lost the ABC War', *The Age*, 4 June 2003; Gerard Henderson, 'Over the Top in the Culture Wars', *The Age*, 14 January 2003.
35 Interview with Andrew Dodd, *The Australian*, 15 March 2001.

36 Imre Salusinszky, 'The Harm Left in Treacherous Thought', *The Australian*, 9 April 2003; Gerard Henderson, 'Rallying Around the Flag is No Jingoism', *Sydney Morning Herald*, 8 April 2003; Letter to the Editor from David Hanson–Levering, *Sydney Morning Herald*, 9 April 2003; Letter to the Editor from Guy Rundle, *The Age*, 10 April 2003.
37 Orwell, 'Notes on nationalism', in *Decline of the English Murder and other essays*, p. 179.
38 Such as *Keep the Aspidistra Flying*, the main character of which, Gordon Comstock, is, like Miller's character, a whoring, penniless writer who has rejected the money god.
39 Orwell, 'Inside the Whale', in *Inside the Whale and other essays*, pp. 10 and 43.
40 Orwell, 'Inside the Whale', in *Inside the Whale and other essays*, p. 47.

Chapter Three

1 Orwell, *The Road to Wigan Pier*, pp. 152–3.
2 George Orwell, 'Why I Write', in *Decline of the English Murder and other essays*, p. 186.
3 Meyers, *Orwell: Wintry Conscience of a Generation*, p. 81.
4 Rob Birrell and Virginia Rapson, 'Two Australias: migrant settlement at the end of the 20th Century', *People and Place*, vol. 10, no. 1, 2002; Katherine Betts, 'Boatpeople and the 2001 Election', *People and Place*, vol. 10, no. 3, 2002.
5 See, for instance, Bob Birrell, 'Australian mothers: fewer and poorer', *People and Place*, vol. 8, no. 2, 2000; Bob Birrell, Kevin O'Connor and Virginia Rapson , 'Explaining spatial concentrations of the poor in metropolitan Melbourne', vol. 7, no. 1, 1999; Bob Birrell, Angelo Calderon and Ian Dobson, 'Equity in access to higher education revisited', *People and Place*, vol. 8, no. 1, 2000.
6 Michael Pusey, *The Experience of Middle Australia: The Dark Side of Economic Reform*, Cambridge University Press, Port Melbourne, 2003, esp. pp. 68–71.
7 Quoted in Meyers, *Orwell: Wintry Conscience of a Generation*, p. 138.
8 Orwell, *The Road to Wigan Pier*, pp. 122 and 112.
9 Orwell, *The Road to Wigan Pier*, p. 15.
10 Orwell, *The Road to Wigan Pier*, p. 16.
11 Orwell, *The Road to Wigan Pier*, p. 16–17.
12 Orwell, *The Road to Wigan Pier*, p. 86.
13 Orwell, *The Road to Wigan Pier*, pp. 47–8.
14 George Orwell, 'The Cost of Letters', *CEJL*, vol. 4, pp. 236–8; Meyers,

Orwell: wintry conscience of a generation, p. 290.
15 Corrie Perkin, *The Age*, 23 June 2002; Letter to the Editor, *The Age*, 30 June 2002.
16 Orwell, *The Road to Wigan Pier*, p. 136.
17 Clive Hamilton, *The Age*, 14 May 2002.
18 Ray Cassin, *The Age*, 19 May 2002.
19 Christopher Hitchens, *Letters to a Young Contrarian*, Basic Books, Cambridge M. A., 2001, p. 3; Christopher Hitchens, *Orwell's Victory*, Allen Lane, London, 2002, p. 4.
20 'Letter to Francis A. Henson', 16 June 1949, *CELJ* 4, p. 564.
21 Orwell, *Nineteen Eighty–Four*, p. 59–60.
22 George Orwell, 'The Lion and the Unicorn', in *CEJL*, vol. 2, p. 78.
23 George Orwell, 'Letter to Julian Symons', 17 September 1949, *CEJL*, vol. 4, p. 570.
24 Orwell, *The Road to Wigan Pier*, pp. 104–5.
25 George Orwell, 'Charles Dickens', in *Decline of the English Murder and other essays*, pp. 138–9.
26 Orwell, 'Charles Dickens', in *Decline of the English Murder and other essays*, pp. 87, 97, 137 and 138.
27 George Orwell, *A Clergyman's Daughter*, Penguin, Harmondsworth, 1990, pp. 118–19.
28 George Orwell, 'Extracts from a manuscript note book', 17 April 1949, *CEJL*, vol. 4, p. 578.
29 Lindy Edwards, *How to Argue with an Economist*, Cambridge University Press, Port Melbourne, 2002, pp. 57–8.
30 Orwell, 'The Lion and the Unicorn', in *CEJL*, vol. 2, p. 108.
31 Orwell, 'The Lion and the Unicorn', in *CEJL*, vol. 2, p. 127.
32 Edmund Campion, 'Wintry Conscience', *Eureka Street*, May 2003, p. 22.
33 Orwell, 'The Lion and the Unicorn', in *CEJL*, vol. 2, p. 88.
34 Quoted in Richard Rorty, *Philosophy and Social Hope*, Penguin, Harmondsworth, 1999, p. 260.
35 Orwell, *The Road to Wigan Pier*, p. 138.
36 Richard Flanagan, 'Election 2001: this is not my Australia', *The Age*, 9 November 2001.
37 Richard Flanagan, *The Australian*, 8 November 1999.
38 Orwell, 'The Lion and the Unicorn', in *CEJL*, vol. 2, pp. 94–5.

Chapter Four

1 George Orwell, 'Writers and Leviathan', in *CEJL*, vol. 4, pp. 468–9.